The SABR Review of Books

A Forum of Baseball Literary Opinion

Volume III - 1988

Edited by **Paul D. Adomites**.

Interior design by and illustrations courtesy of **John Thorn**.

NOTE ON THE COVER: The art for the cover, by Edgar Keller, is part of a Library of Congress publication -- *Facsimile of Casey at the Bat*, which includes the poem, illustrations and a record of DeWolf Hopper reciting the poem in 1909. It can be purchased at the Library, or by writing: Information Office, Box A, Library of Congress, Washington DC 20540. Price is $5.95 plus $2 postage and handling.

The SABR Review of Books

Table of Contents

SPECIAL FEATURE

PERSONAL FAVORITE

THE SABR REVIEW OF BOOKS, VOLUME 3, 1988. (ISBN 0-910137-33-1, ISSN 0888-8124). Published by the Society for American Baseball Research, Inc., P.O. Box 10033, Kansas City MO 64111. Postage paid at Pittsburgh, PA 15233. Copyright © 1988, Society for American Baseball Research, Inc. All rights reserved. Reproduction in whole or in part without written permission is prohibited. Printed by Mathews Graphics Corporation, Pittsburgh, PA.

Editor's Notes

Horton Publishing Company (P.O. Box 29234, St. Louis MO, 63126) is continuing their wonderful reprint series of *Spalding Official Guides*. Now available, 1884 through 1888, plus the format-changing 1889 (full color cover, photos inside.) $14.95 plus $2 P&H for each...More great reprints. SABR member Jeffrey Neuman has moved from his editor's post at Macmillan to Director of Sports Books at Simon & Schuster, where he's currently focusing on reviving some baseball (and other sports) classics. How's this for a start? Pat Jordan's *A False Spring*, Roger Angell's *Five Seasons*, and John Underwood/Ted Williams' *My Turn at Bat*. (See page 31.) To come are *A Donald Honig Reader* and more. Good job, Jeff.

In the abbreviated review department, Merritt Clifton had this to say about Tim McCarver's *Oh Baby, I Love It!* (Villard Books, Random House, $16.95): "If books could be printed on polyester, this would be a leisure suit in a second rate chain department store."...Darlene Ann Mehrer read *Runs, Hits and Errors*, Jim Langford's compilation of Cub history and humor, (Diamond Communications, $14.95) and said that even though she liked Jim's first book on the subject, *The Game is Never Over*, she felt his newer effort was too often repetitive of the older...Another book from Diamond Communications, *Legends of Baseball; An Oral History of the Game's Golden Age* ($8.95) was described as "the perfect book to take to the beach for some fun reading" by Frank Boslett. He particularly liked the Carl Hubbell interview ("quite a different picture of McGraw than we saw in *The Glory of Their Times*.")...If you like the cartoon "Shoe" and relate to the Cubs' fans' predicament, you'll get a kick out of *How Many Next Years Do You Get in Baseball: Shoe Goes to Wrigley Field* (Bonus Books, $5.95). The segment on the "Metaphor Abuse Hotline" is my favorite.

A confessed all-star junkie, Philip Bergen took a close look at *Baseball's All-Star Game: A Game-By-Game Guide* by Jeff Lenburg (Jefferson, NC: McFarland & Co.). Unfortunately he found it full of errors: "The 1936 game was played at Braves Field, not Fenway Park; the 1958 game was not played at night; Lou Gehrig presumably did not have 149 rbi's by the All-Star break in 1937" and more...However, another McFarland book, *Sports Films: A Complete Reference*, by Zucker and Babich, certainly seems to live up to its title: 33 pages on baseball movies, with 416 pages overall (more than 2000 films). Fun to look through, a genuine killer for trivia -- $39.95 from McFarland, Box 611, Jefferson NC 28640...Jack Lang sends along a brief note on Noel Hynd's *The Giants of the Polo Grounds*: "The book is so full of errors I gave up reading it."

A work which would have been included in Dick Beverage's Minor League Literature survey (had it arrived in time) is Stew Thornley's lively *On to Nicollet*, the story of the glory and fame of the Minneapolis Miners. It's available from Nodin Press, Minneapolis for $9.95.

As always *The SABR Review* fights a deadline and loses. Books which arrived too late to review this time around: Joe Garagiola's *It's Anybody's Ballgame*,

Ozzie Smith's *Wizard*, Jack McKeon's *Jack of All Trades*, W.P. Kinsella's book of short stories, *The Further Adventures of Slugger McBatt*, and John Thorn's impressive-looking *The Game for All America*. The deadline prevented a feature on books by pitchers (Ryan, McLain, Hunter), too. Thanks to Tom Jozwik, Scott Bushnell and Irwin Chusid for writing articles which space just couldn't squeeze in.

And thanks to all of you for being so supportive and making this job so much fun.

NEW YORK, SATURDAY JULY 2, 1870.

BASE BALL CELEBRITIES.

GEORGE WRIGHT, Short Stop of the Cincinnati Club. DICK McBRIDE, Captain and Pitcher of the Philadelphia Athletic Club,

Contributors

ELIOT COHEN is an editor of *Who's Who in Baseball* and editor/publisher of the outspoken baseball newsletter, *Major League Monthly*...LUKE SALISBURY'S book on baseball, trivia, and life, *Baseball Catechism*, will be published this year by Times Books.

GEORGE ROBINSON writes regularly on sports for United Features Syndicate and for Newspaper Enterprise Association, and is associate editor of The Main Event, a monthly sports magazine for doctors. He is currently working on a book about behind-the-scenes people in major league baseball.

PHILIP BERGEN is a professional librarian, and compiler of the two indices to SABR publications...DICK JOHNSON is director of programs for the New England Sports Museum... BILL JAMES is the author of the award-winning *Bill James Historical Baseball Abstract*.

ED GOLDSTEIN is a partner in the world's "most mixed marriage -- a Jewish Democrat Yankee fan to a Catholic Republican Dodger fan.''... MERRITT CLIFTON is editor and publisher of Samisdat Press...DAVID L. ULIN lives in New York City. He writes a monthly column for *Cover* magazine and recently completed his first novel.

A SABR board member from 1983-88, TOM JOZWIK has written about baseball for Milwaukee area newspapers and the Associated Press, as well as for SABR publications...FREDERICK IVOR-CAMPBELL'S brief biography of Henry Chadwick, published in *Harvard Magazine*, has been picked up by the USIA for republication overseas.

JOE OVERFIELD is the author of the classic *100 Seasons of Buffalo Baseball*, and is the historian for the Buffalo baseball club...BILL BORST, "The Baseball Professor," is an author, historian, radio and TV personality and founder of the St. Louis Browns Fan Club...DARLENE MEHRER is the founder and editor of *Basewoman*.

GLENN STOUT is librarian at the Boston Public Library and unofficial curator of the "Boston Tradition in Sports" collection...DICK BEVERAGE is a long-suffering Cubs fan and author of two books on the Pacific Coast League -- *Hollywood Stars* and *Los Angeles Angels*.

LOUIS RUBIN is the editorial director of Algonquin Books of Chapel Hill, and University Distinguished Professor of English at University of North Carolina there...PETE CAVA is press information director of the Athletics Congress for the U.S., America's governing body for track and field.

JOE DOBROW has worked at public relations on the agency, corporate, and non-profit sides. He is currently PR director for the New England Sports Museum...JIM SUMNER works in the archaeology and historical preservation section of the North Carolina Department of Public Resources... FRANK BOSLETT is an avid raconteur.

PETER BJARKMAN, who is also called "The Baseball Professor," is a baseball historian and freelance writer interested in baseball literature (especially fiction.)...JERRY TOMLINSON is author of the invaluable SABR publication, *The Baseball Research Handbook*...LEN LEVIN is a Providence, RI-based writer and editor.

Where Baseball Literature Begins

By Glenn Stout

BASEBALL LITERATURE BEGINS WITH "CASEY AT The Bat."

While Ernest L. Thayer's classic verse is neither the first poem to utilize baseball as its subject, nor the first attempt to capture the game under the guise of literature, "Casey At The Bat", one hundred years after its first appearance, remains the most memorable piece of baseball writing ever produced. No subsequent poem, column, short story or novel approaches "Casey" for its ability to delineate our attraction toward the game.

It is easily the best remembered poem, on any subject, ever written by an American author. Very few of us, upon hearing the first line "The outlook wasn't brilliant for the Mudville nine that day," can fail to supply the remainder of the opening stanza, regardless of the depth of our own, individual baseball knowledge. If one's familiarity with the game is limited to only a single experience, that experience is likely to be "Casey At The Bat." A few months ago, in baseball-savvy Boston, someone actually asked me, with complete and utter sincerity, "Who's Ted Williams?"

A few weeks later, recovered from my initial shock and having sufficiently recast my world view to allow for such a question to be asked, I once again cautiously turned our conversation toward baseball, this time evoking simply the name "Casey" and the place "Mudville."

To my delight she responded with the poem's opening words. I exhaled a deep sigh of relief and went on to wax rhapsodic over my own peculiar fascination with the poem. Of course, I haven't seen her since, but my faith in "Casey" continues unabated.

What I still find curious is that despite the poem's popularity, and despite its central position in the literature of an essential experience of American culture, "Casey" is entirely ignored in the study of American literature. Now that's not all bad, for academia has ground enough good literature to dust in its gristmill of analysis, but completely to overlook "Casey" seems almost sinister, part of some conspiracy to belittle not only baseball, but all that it inspires, as if our affection for the poem and for the game it describes is some kind of dirty little secret unworthy of public scrutiny.

In this instance, I'm one of the unashamed, maddened thousands yelling "Fraud!" "Casey At The Bat" does not belong in any literary bush league. The poem deserves attention proportionate with our affection for it. In its own way "Casey" is no less a work of original American literature than Whitman's "Song of Myself," or Kerouac's "On the Road." It defines a part of what we are, something uniquely American, and points out something universal and essential in all our lives. Casey's struggle is our own, and Ernest L. Thayer's ability to point this out is more art than accident. Casey, presumably, came through in the clutch many other times, and failed only in the scenario described by Thayer, while Thayer himself, something of a banjo hitter in the ongoing league of literature, rose to the occasion only once and knocked the cover off the ball with "Casey." A happy coincidence perhaps, but the run still counts.

The source of the poem's success and subsequent staying power stems from the congruence between the poem's subject - baseball, and its form, the ballad. Thayer himself once told a reporter that "I evolved 'Casey' from the situation I had seen so often in baseball, a crack batsman coming to bat with the bases filled, and then fallen down." Unwittingly perhaps, Thayer chose to write about the game's most dramatic confrontation, the nearly archetypal contest, with the game in balance, between the pitcher and the batter, the batter and himself, the crowd and the unfolding drama, between the individual who seeks to control his own fate and the forces that try to deny that possibility. The symbolic nature of this universal confrontation makes the poem at once eternal and immediate. Very few of us have not had backyard dreams of coming to the plate in a similar situation, and very few of us have not faced precisely the same confrontation elsewhere. In an American context, the confrontation delicately probes one of our most precious myths, whether the individual can make a difference and find expression within a larger sphere. Thayer acknowledges this and even subtitles the poem "A Ballad of the Republic." Casey's on-field struggle takes place simultaneously in both a human and political dimension. We cannot help but become engaged by Casey's plight, for Casey is one of us.

With such heady stuff at stake, Thayer's wise use of the ballad form stakes the conflict to the ground and allows easy access to its narrative explication. The poem's thirteen, four-line stanzas, all following the same basic scheme of rhyme and rhythm, are so transparent and simple that the active voice of the poem, Casey actually at the bat, comes through uncluttered. Where most parodies of Casey fail is in their struggle to duplicate Thayer's nearly invisible form, twisting the language to fit a pattern that will never work as well again. In Thayer's poem, the form all but disappears after one or two readings. Thayer's detailed combination of baseball terminology and idiom all slide nicely into place and the story lays out like a line score in the morning paper.

Now this was no poetic breakthrough on Thayer's part. The ballad form dominated American newspaper verse, and "Casey At The Bat," which first appeared on June 3, 1888 in the *San Francisco Examiner*, is not unlike thousands of other poems that similarly found their way into print. Yet Thayer's language, drawn from the game itself and its 1880 environs, manages to pull off a highly musical and nearly seamless coupling between word, rhythm, and rhyme that lifts it from the ordinary and forgettable and lets its other elements - drama and metaphor - extend beyond the imposed structure. Ultimately, the poem's form, by way of its transparency, releases far more than it restricts.

In the first stanza, Thayer writes perhaps the greatest lead in all of baseball literature. The cumulative efforts of the Baseball Writers Association of America have yet to do as well as Thayer. In four short lines he tells the reader all he needs to know about the situation at hand - two outs, two runs down, and, apparently little hope left anywhere. By fixing the poem securely within a baseball game situation, and never straying from the drama of the moment, he allows the poem's symbolic elements to develop organically, from the play of the game itself, and never appear forced or contrived.

Perhaps this is why "Casey" has never been the subject of any intense scrutiny apart from its own genealogy in American culture. For "Casey," because it is written for a baseball audience and is so unquestionably "about" baseball, does not provide a convenient handle, outside the game itself, for further analysis. Much modern baseball poetry, the bulk of which I find pretty good, still often errs in leaping too quickly to the symbol and straying from the game itself. "Casey," on the other hand, keeps its head, and heart, in the center of the diamond. It is primarily a game report, and its significance beyond that stems from the integrity of Thayer's initial reportage.

Almost effortlessly, Thayer positions the character of the mighty Casey as the heroic, isolated individual, alone against the impersonal demands of fate. "Mighty Casey" is clearly the greatest hitter the denizens of Mudville have ever known. He identifies Casey's team, the "Mudville nine," and several teammates, Anglo/Irish everymen Cooney, Barrows, Flynn and Blake, but every other figure in the narrative, the crowd, the umpire, and the pitcher, is left a complete blank. Only Casey develops a personality.

As individual readers of the poem, we identify with Casey because there is, quite literally, no one else there. He has no peer.

In human contrast to Casey the individual, is the crowd, an emotional, murmuring, mass of mankind shaped from the clays of Mudville that Thayer uses like a mirror on which to project our fears over the potential loss of individuality. The crowd is constantly referred to in a series of nouns and phrases that are ever more indistinct and unsavory - "the straggling few...in deep despair," "the rest," "the stricken multitude," "5,000 throats," "the maddened thousands" and so forth. In 1888 America was in the midst of an industrial revolution that was quickly becoming increasingly dehumanizing, and Thayer's desultory crowd seems plucked from the darkness of some roaring industrial nightmare. Only Casey's appearance following the clutch hitting of Flynn and Blake inspires them and is able to replace "grim melancholy" with the "lusty yell" of faith.

Casey's appearance in the poem's sixth stanza draws focus away from the larger game situation and corresponding crowd reaction and concentrates it on his individual plight. The crowd identifies with Casey. Like a conquering hero he has advanced, not simply walked, to the plate, and stands there, preening, acknowledging the cheers of the crowd for whom he is king.

What follows is the greatest at-bat in the history of baseball. Forget Ruth's "called shot" off Charlie Root. That may well be nothing more than myth. Casey's at-bat takes place before the multitudes. Watched by "ten thousand eyes" and applauded by "five thousand tongues," Casey stands alone "in haughty grandeur" to take his licks against the onslaught of fate. On the mound is a demonic, faceless "writhing pitcher," evil personified, and behind the plate his partner, the austere and emotionless umpire. Together, they act in consort with one another to try to deny Casey his opportunity to strike a blow for the common man. They control the ball, and only by supreme force of will can Casey wrest his destiny from their hands and send it skyward, into the crowd and out of reach of the powers that be. Ruth never knew this much pressure.

When Casey watches the first pitch sail by and states unequivocally "That ain't my style," he speaks in the language of everyone who has ever felt manipulated and powerless. When the umpire unemotionally calls "Strike one," the people react accordingly. Yelling "Kill the umpire!" in the face of the arbiter's presumably biased and detached judgment is nothing less than a call for revolution. Casey does not concede defeat, but counter-attacks with a "smile of Christian charity," enforcing his moral superiority against the unfolding conspiracy.

When the second pitch, another ball, is also called a strike, the crowd again threatens to turn violent, calling out "Fraud!" and apparently recognizing the inherent injustice of Casey's struggle in a game so patently unfair. Yet once more, Casey stills the crowd.

This time he reacts not with moral superiority, for that is of little use in a battle that is taking place outside moral boundaries, but with brute, physical force. His face turns "stern and cold," "his muscles strain," his "teeth are clenched in hate," and his bat turns into a club of "cruel violence." The frustrations of the crowd have become Casey's. He is them, and has become an expression of the animal that remains in man, the dark, violent underside that inequity and inequality can call to the fore. He succumbs to the call of the crowd and becomes pure symbol. At this moment Casey is no longer a lone batsman swinging at a ball to win some game, or merely a solitary figure, in eternal struggle to take hold of his own destiny. He becomes a representation of a larger, collective call for the emergence of the pure, brute force of human will.

The poem's rhythm, reinforced by recurring internal rhyme, builds to a fever pitch as "now the pitcher holds the ball, and now he lets it go,/ and now the air is shattered by the force of Casey's blow." exploding magnificently in a moment of pure epiphany as everything in the poem reaches its climax.

But we all know what happened next. Casey struck no blow for all mankind, banged no four-bagger into a mass of screaming hands. Hell, he didn't even foul the damn pitch off. All he hit was air. Thayer withdraws to utter a wistful, rhyming "Oh," and in that quiet, forgiving, single syllable, begins to draw a picture of a softer, brighter, more optimistic world that we almost forgot in our frenzy over Casey's fate. Somewhere else, things are better. Perhaps the powers-that-be are not the devil incarnate. Time goes on, the sun still shines, the band still plays, and the laughing of man and the shouts of children creep back into the consciousness. To Ernest L. Thayer, there's a Norman Rockwell world waiting out there someplace.

"There is no joy in Mudville," but Thayer has already taken us away from that memorable place. "Casey has struck out," and must remain there forever, defeated and alone to nurse his wounds in private, but by allowing us to leave Mudville Thayer leaves open the possibility that somewhere else, sometime, a different conclusion might be reached. Only Casey has struck out. We live on to come to bat again. In Casey's one, great swing, baseball becomes a game again.

And that is probably the one, great lesson that comes from "Casey At The Bat." Baseball, no matter how it affects us and no matter how much time and serious attention we give it, no matter what happens, in spite of everything we do to mess it up, somehow stays a game. And it doesn't matter if Thayer had this in mind or not when he sat down and wrote the poem, anymore than it matters how baseball was born or why it works. Just be glad it does, and enjoy it for that. Baseball can mean what we want it to, but it can never be anything else. All I know is that one hundred years from now, unless we mess up the world completely, baseball will still be here and "Casey At The Bat" will still be read and celebrated. If that happens, perhaps Thayer will be proven correct. In another place, in another time, maybe one of us will tear the cover off the ball.

Mudville might win yet, and the girl who asked me about Ted Williams could still come back.

A Survey of Minor League Literature

By Dick Beverage

IF YOU SPENT MOST OF YOUR FORMATIVE YEARS IN Nebraska, as I did, the major leagues were like a fairy tale. In the late 40's and early 50's the closest major league park was in St. Louis. Harry Caray's voice filled the evening air in those days, and most people were Cardinal fans, if anything. There were exceptions, of course. I was a Cub fan, thanks to listening to Bert Wilson during the afternoons of the summer of 1948. My real penchant for masochism clearly manifested itself that season, as the Cubs finished last and I loved them.

The real game in town, however, was found in Omaha Municipal Stadium, where the Western League Cardinals operated. Good baseball was played there. The home team wore uniforms which were identical to those of their famous parent, and when the Des Moines Bruins came to town, wearing Cub hand-me-downs, it was St. Louis and Chicago all over again. But that was imaginary. Our Cardinals were real. We thrilled to the heroics of Ed Lewinski and Larry Miggins; wait till these guys get to St. Louis! Stan Musial and Enos Slaughter, you better look out. I loved it when the Lincoln Athletics came to town with big Lou Limmer at first base. He was from New York, too. Talked funny, didn't he, when he signed your autograph book. I bet he'll be great when he gets to Connie Mack's team. Look at Bobby Shantz. He made it, and Limmer will be there next year, just wait and see.

This was real baseball as far as I was concerned. I had spent the summer of 1946 in California and there discovered the Pacific Coast League. There was a real major league. Yes, they're better than our Western League boys, but not much. Every now and then a Western Leaguer would go out to the Coast — Cliff Aberson did that and played well. And don't forget the Kansas City Blues. We could hear their games once in a while if you adjusted your radio just so. The American Association sounded okay. Maybe, next year we'll go down for a Blues game.

My experiences were not unique. There is a hard core of West Coast fans who are resentful to this day that the Dodgers and Giants displaced the PCL Angels, Stars and Seals. An annual reunion of Newark Bear alumni and fans draws a sizeable turnout. The Rochester Red Wings have had a solid following. Clearly, the interest in the minor leagues runs strong and deep.

Yet, the amount of literature on the minor leagues does not reflect that involvement. I think that this is partly a result of geography. The great publishing houses of the nation center around New York, where awareness of the minor leagues, let alone interest, hardly exists. This seems to have always been true.

The minors have always been viewed negatively, as a troublesome part of Organized Baseball, and what writing there was merely reinforced that notion. As early as May, 1913 William Phelon asked, "What are we going to do about the minor leagues?" in *Baseball Magazine*. "What's the Matter with the Minor Leagues?" by Ed Barrow merely rephrased that question four years later in the same publication. And E.S. Barnard wanted to know, "What is wrong with Minor League Baseball?" in November, 1930.

The answer to that question should have been, "Nothing." Minor league baseball was great and enjoyed by those who watched it. You just couldn't read much about it outside of *The Sporting News*, which faithfully tabulated the results and printed all the gossip. The first book which dealt with the minor leagues, according to the Grobani *Guide to Baseball Literature*, was *History of the National Association of Professional Baseball Leagues* by John Foster. This was a brief history of the minor leagues printed by the National Association office in 1926 and is rare today. The Pacific Coast League put out an annual record book compiled by league statistician Leo Moriarty during the '20s, but these were limited in scope. In 1932, William Ruggles produced his *History of the Texas League* in his role as secretary of that distinguished circuit.

What I would consider the first real book on minor league baseball was published in early 1939, and it was original for its day. Fred Lange was a native of the San Francisco Bay Area who had played in the Western League during the 1887-88 seasons. Like so many Californians, he could not leave his native habitat and gave up a promising career to go into business in Oakland. But he remained a keen observer of the baseball scene, and at the age of sixty-nine, published his memories under the title, *History of Baseball in California and Pacific Coast Leagues 1847-1938 — Memories and Musings of an Old Time Player*.

Lange's history is an important document. He covers baseball on the Pacific Coast from its inception and does so in such a way that the reader feels a sense of being there. As Lange ages, his descriptions of events are not quite as sharp, but they are still revealing. The bulk of the book is focused on the Pacific Coast League from its beginning in 1903 through the 1938 season. While Lange doesn't devote much space to the events of each· season, he includes biographical sketches of PCL luminaries throughout. The tone is strictly conversational. You learn that Jimmy Reese is engaged to marry the daughter of the Emeryville police chief, and Lange suggests that you stop by Reese's restaurant for "good eats." Ernie Lombardi is still living in his childhood home and has two lovely sisters who are very proud of him.

There are some minor spelling inaccuracies, but generally speaking, Lange's memories are reliable, and he used the newspapers to check most of his facts. As a result, the book is an invaluable source for the PCL historian. Unfortunately, it was privately published and copies are not easily found today.

During the post World War II period, a number of publications were issued by the various leagues. These tended to be of the record book variety for the most part. Some clubs issued yearbooks in the fashion of the major leagues. Probably the best of this type of publication were the Rollie Truitt Portland Beaver yearbooks, which were full of pictures and statistics. The American Association had its own version of Who's Who in Baseball during the 1947-51 seasons. Packed with photographs, these jewels were impressively done.

In 1952 the National Association commemorated its golden anniversary by publishing *The Story of Minor League Baseball*. If the earlier version was too short, this 742-page volume more than corrected that oversight. It was prepared by Robert Finch, L.H. Addington and Edward Morgan. Finch and Addington had long associations with the minor league offices. Addington was Judge Bramham's assistant for many years, while Finch was the National Association secretary for a spell. The book consists of a historical section on the National Association written by Finch and Addington and an extensive compilation of league records which was prepared by Morgan. There is very little that he left out. The record holders by league, outstanding performance by individual players, managers who made good in the majors--all of this information can be found here. A detailed index is provided as well.

I find this book to be very useful for the researcher as well as the general minor league fan. Some of the work is now dated, and there are errors in some of the numbers. It is essentially a political work, if a baseball book can be described as such. The National Association was a very fragile institution in the early '50's, and the issuance of *The Story of Minor League*

Baseball is partially designed to remind Organized Baseball in general how important the minor league structure was to the game. The book does not seem to be wholly intended for the general public, and a limited number of copies were published.

As important as the publication of *The Story of Minor League Baseball* was to minor league literature, the landmark book is *Bush League* by Robert Obojski. Published in 1974, it is the first history of the minors to be given mass circulation. Like Gaul, *Bush League* is divided into three parts. Part 1 gives a history of the minors from 1877 to date in a two-chapter overview. In this section are included individual sections on the important contributions of Branch Rickey, Frank Shaughnessy and George Weiss to the minor leagues. Part 2 is devoted to individual histories of the high minor leagues with yearly highlights, league champions and records. Obojski also profiles the Middle Atlantic League, which he considers the toughest Class C league in history.

Part 3 deals with several of the great minor league players; the feats of Joe Hauser and Ike Boone are given prominence. Then there are listings of outstanding accomplishments and all of the cities known to have fielded minor league teams. Vern Luse has enlarged this list in recent years.

One of the fine features of *Bush League* is its upbeat tone. For the first time, we have a book that is positive about the minors. Obojski praises the leagues and the players and clearly shows how important the minor leagues are to baseball history. I think it fair to credit the book with much of the increased interest in the minors since that time. It has led to the publication of much fine work on the minors.

Generally speaking, books on minor league baseball fall into one of two categories. They are either a history or nostalgic look at specific leagues and clubs, or they are descriptions by players of life as a minor league player. Of the latter, the message is always the same. We were young, it was tough riding the buses, we drank a lot and played practical jokes on each other, and we worked hard to get out of there. Sometimes we made the majors, sometimes we didn't. And we almost always started in Class D.

The classic of this type is *A False Spring* by Pat Jordan. It is the story of a high school phenom who played three years in the Braves' farm system beginning in 1959. Jordan was a bonus baby and as such, rated a little higher on the totem pole than some of his teammates. But he still had to suffer the same experiences as the rest.

Jordan is an exceptional writer, and his skill in painting word pictures of the teams, the players and the surroundings make this book the model of its type. It is not so much about minors as it is about a boy growing up. McCook, Davenport, Waycross--they're all well described, and you understand what it must have been like in the lower minors almost thirty years ago.

At the other end of the spectrum is *Low and Outside--The True Confessions of a Minor League Player* by Jerry Kettle. This is everything that *A False Spring* is not. It is badly written and careless with detail; Kettle can't seem to get anyone's name right. Manager Benny Zientara becomes Vinny Zintera; Bill Posedel is Bill Fosdel. The least his editor could do is look up the names. Kettle comes across as a cocky unpleasant jock, and inspires no sympathy when his career is shortened by an arm injury. Kettle played in the Phillies system, and life in Mattoon, Tifton, and High Point-Thomasville is not much different from McCook.

Somewhat in between these two is *What's a Nice Harvard Boy Like You Doing in the Bushes?* by Rick Wolff. Wolff, the son of announcer Bob Wolff, graduated magna cum laude from Harvard in 1973 and spent the next two years as a Tiger farmhand. Anderson, South Carolina and Clinton, Iowa are the locales featured here. Wolff focuses on the camaraderie he found with his teammates and does a reasonably good job. The book is a bit of a lightweight, however, and I expected more, considering the Ivy League background.

Of similar quality is *Five Straight Errors on Ladies Day* by Walter Nagel. This is a reminiscence of the author's career of his early days in the Pacific Coast League. Nagel played at Los Angeles and Portland in the 1905-07 era and had a brief major league career with Pittsburgh and the Red Sox. The book is really oral history, written almost sixty years after the events. The most interesting discovery is how Walter Johnson almost became an Angel.

Don Honig used his formidable interviewing skills to produce *Up From the Minors* in 1970, but his book falls below his usual standards. Seven prominent major leaguers of the time, including Pete Rose and Tom Seaver, recount their experiences in the minors. The accounts are very reasoned and articulate but lack any real vitality; the exceptions are Bobby Bonds and Reggie Smith. Each had the additional burden of being a young black in the South during his first year in Organized Baseball. One would think that the Giants and Red Sox would be a bit more sensitive to the problems these young players faced.

In 1984 Marc Gunther used much the same approach in *Basepaths*. It is the story of careers from the lower minors up through the majors and beyond. The author interviews a different player at each step and then summarizes each career in his epilogue. The emphasis in this book is on career development, not life in the minors itself. A good book, though, and well worth reading.

Like two peas in a pod are *Wait Till I Make the Show* by Bob Ryan and *Beating the Bushes* by Frank Dolson. The books were written by two excellent sportswriters eight years apart, using the same format. They traveled with minor league teams to get a real flavor of life in the minor leagues. Curiously, Jim Bunning's career as a manager in the Phillies system is featured in both books. Dolson's was written in 1982, a bit longer and confined to the Phillies farms as one would expect from his Philadelphia *Inquirer* background. Ryan's book features a wonderful description of the Termite Palace in Honolulu, where the Islanders played. If ever a park resembled Sulphur Dell in Nashville, this was it. I think that Dolson is the better of the two. Wonder if we'll complete this trilogy in 1990?

Worthy of note is *Baseball and the Cold War* by Howard Senzel. This is an unusual book, somewhat autobiographical, which focuses on the infamous shooting incident at Havana in 1959. There manager Frank Verdi of the Rochester Red Wings was wounded by a shot fired by a Castro minion at a Sugar King game.

Senzel grew up in Rochester, found baseball as a boy, abandoned it during the 60's when he became a radical, and then returns to the game in 1975 by reliving the events of the shooting. He realizes that baseball is his rod and his staff. Sounds like a SABR member to me.

I think that the best writing on the minors falls into the league and team history category. It is not surprising, considering that some of the most illustrious SABR members have produced work in this area--Joe Overfield, Ralph LinWeber, Jim Bready, Arthur Schott. The International League has generated the most coverage by far. However, there are some excellent books on several other leagues.

The best of these histories is Overfield's *The 100 Seasons of Buffalo Baseball*. It covers the entire history of the Bisons, including their years in the National League, concluding with the 1984 season. Each year is given its own summary chapter and statistics. There are numerous photographs (including several action shots in Offermann Stadium), the great Bisons are profiled, and the importance of the club to the community is given much attention. The advantage that the author has over most minor league historians is his long association with the team. He saw his first Bison game in 1925, and with time out for World War II service, has been a faithful supporter ever since. He personally saw most of the greats and was an official of the community-owned Bisons of the '50s; this gives his history an authenticity that is lacking in others. It's an outstanding history of a ball club and could hardly be improved upon.

Two excellent histories of the Newark Bears have been produced by SABR members. Randy Linthurst produced a three volume set--*Newark*

Bears; *Newark Bears-The Middle Years*; and *Newark Bears-The Final Years*. They cover the Bears from 1931, when the club was purchased by Colonel Ruppert and the Yankees through the final season of 1949. It's a year-by-year account of the club and naturally concentrates on the great 1937 team. The author provides an abundance of pictures and includes correspondence from former players and fans. The books are small, about one hundred pages each, and could have easily been consolidated into one. Linthurst presents a very thoughtful analysis of the decline and fall of the Newark franchise, giving as reasons (beyond the obvious impact of television) decline of the park neighborhood, the Yankees' need to stock the Kansas City franchise, the recall of Bob Porterfield in 1948.

Ron Mayer's well-illustrated book, *The 1937 Newark Bears*, provides more extensive detail on the 1937 season and the careers of the players. He begins his account with the 1932 season, building up to the championship year. A capsule biography of each of the key Bears is included, and there is good statistical information along with an index. Mayer includes a virtual play-by-play of the Junior World Series with Columbus where the Bears came from three games behind to win the championship; this is the most exciting part of the season. A very well-written book.

The Canadian members of the International League receive attention in Bill Humber's *Cheering for the Home Team*. Although this book is not exclusively about the minors, it is an historical overview of baseball in Canada and naturally devotes much attention to the Canadian minor league teams. A more complete report on the Toronto Maple Leafs is found in *Baseball's Back in Town*, by Louis Cauz. This book was issued in 1977 to commemorate the creation of the Toronto Blue Jays.

Cauz has produced a very fine book. Its emphasis is on the Maple Leafs, and the history of that club is presented in a summary form, decade by decade. The photographs in this book are remarkable. There are pictures of all of the Toronto ballparks, team pictures, good action shots and prominent Maple Leafs, some of which are in color. No statistics to speak of, but there is a brief bibliography. The photography by itself makes this one a great buy.

Jim Bready profiles the minor league Orioles in *The Home Team*, a history of baseball in Baltimore from 1858. This small volume of 124 pages allocates a mere nine pages to the minor league team, but they are good ones. Bready includes several good mini-biographies of the stars of the 1919-25 pennant winners along with many rare photographs. Although I enjoyed this book very much, I think the author could have given more space to the International League team. After all, Baltimore was a league member for 51 years.

The successor team to the Orioles, the Richmond Virginians, is memorialized by Elliott Irving in *Remembering the Vees*. This is a history of the club during the 1954-64 period before it became the Richmond Braves. The author gives a brief year-by-year account and then adds a unique touch by reporting on the post-playing careers of the Vees. He tracked down everyone who played for the Virginians to learn of their post-playing careers. He received responses from virtually every player, and these vignettes fill almost two-thirds of the book. There are many photographs, but the quality of reproduction is not good.

It seems that International League fans had love affairs with their teams. Joe Overfield had his with the Bisons, and John Remington had a similar relationship with the Rochester Red Wings. His *The Red Wings--A Love Affair* is a short nostalgic piece on his favorite team. This book resembles a yearbook in its format, and concentrates on the many fine players who were Red Wings over the years. The great championship teams of 1929-31 are highlighted, and there are many pictures. Remington relied heavily on a previous book *Rochester Diamond Echoes*, which was more detailed. He could have included more statistics.

A definitive history of the International League has yet to be written. Although David Chrisman made an effort to do so in his three volume *History of the International League 1919-60*, he falls well short of the mark. The series is a year-by-year compendium of the league results. The lineup of each club, the pitching staffs and the position in the league standings are recapped, and a brief description of the pennant race is given. At the end of Volume Three an appendix lists the league leaders in the various categories. The books are useful for quick reference, but there are numerous factual errors which severely detract from the work. The most egregious mistake is identifying first baseman Iggy Walters of the 1939 Syracuse Chiefs as Bucky Walters during the finest season of the Reds' pitcher's career! The author seemed to recap the player names from the Guides without regard to who they really were; they are simply names in type and as lifeless as names in a property tax ledger.

This is a case of a self-published book strongly in need of editorial assistance. The many errors should have been caught, and if they had been, the series would have been far more useful. Chrisman is at his best when dealing in general descriptions. The sections on the great Oriole teams of the '20s and the Red Wings of 1929-31 are well done.

In contrast to the abundance of work on the International League, the other two Triple A leagues are not well covered at all. There is no general history on either the American Association or the Pacific Coast League, and team histories are few. Of the original members of the Association, which was the most stable of minor leagues, only Toledo and Louisville can boast of their own history. Ralph LinWeber produced his *Toledo Baseball Guide* in 1943; A.H. Tarvin authored *75 Years on Louisville Diamonds* in 1940. Obviously, both works need considerable updating.

One of the newer Association clubs has its own history, however, and it is a good one. Mark Foster's *The Denver Bears* covers the history of baseball in Denver from its earliest days through the 1982 season. Most of the attention is given to the Bears in the post World War II period as members of the Western League, the American Association and a five year sojourn in the Pacific Coast League. Foster is a Professor of History at the University of Colorado at Denver, and his work reflects his profession. It is well-researched and well-written without the pedantry that is sometimes found in baseball books by scholars. The book contains many fine photographs, including a large number of action shots. The bibliography is somewhat lacking, and the author could have included more player profiles and statistics.

The Pacific Coast League is also lacking a general history. In 1984 Ken Stadler wrote his memoirs in *The Pacific Coast League--One Man's Memories*. Stadler grew up in Los Angeles during the '30s and '40s, where he was a devout fan of the Hollywood Stars. He began watching the games in 1938, when the Stars first came to town, and stayed with them through the 1957 season, their last. Much of the book is devoted to life at Gilmore Field from the viewpoint of the fan. The author gives the reader a real feel for the park, the players and the era. Stadler relies very heavily on his memory, which at times is faulty. Nevertheless, this is a very useful little book, which gives a good overview of the PCL.

It isn't often that a reviewer has the opportunity to mention his own books, but this report would not be complete were I to omit discussion of *The Angels-Los Angeles in the Pacific Coast League 1919-57* and *The Hollywood Stars-Baseball in Movieland 1926-57*. These two books are informal histories of the two Southern California clubs in the Pacific Coast League and have been reviewed elsewhere. They preceded the Stadler book and were the first works on the PCL since Lange's work in 1938.

Just off the presses is Gary Waddingham's *The Seattle Rainiers 1938-42*. This is a detailed account of the best years in the history of that franchise, beginning with the year that Emil Sick bought the decrepit Seattle Indians and saw them win three straight pennants in 1939-41. Waddingham was there for many of those games but relies on his research rather than his memory. There are a few pictures and season statistics. The last chapter is the best. The author recounts what it was like to attend a ball game in Seattle during the summer of 1941. It's an extremely vivid recreation and worth the price of the book by itself.

The Texas League has been blessed with two fine league histories, which were written fifty five years apart. William Ruggles was the Texas League statistician beginning in 1920, and he made the league his life's work. His *History of the Texas League* was first published in 1932 and revised through the 1950 season. An official publication of the league itself, the book is a year-by-year history with an incredible amount of detail. Complete rosters are shown for each club and each year as well as listings of all the managers and umpires. In addition, there is a complete alphabetical player index and many team pictures. It's a tremendous source for the Texas League researcher.

It would seem difficult to improve on Ruggles' work, but Bill O'Neal has done just that. He commemorates the league's centennial with *The Texas League--A Century of Baseball 1888-1987*. This book should be used as a model for other league histories. It gives a decade-by-decade account of the Texas League as a whole, then follows with brief histories of each of the clubs. The author includes a section on the ball parks and profiles the great players. As a grand finale, he includes an appendix which lists the league leaders year by year in all major categories. As part of his work, O'Neal visited each of the league cities and many of the old ball park sites. He is a third generation Texas League fan who probably knows the league better than anyone ever did. Simply an exceptional bit of history.

Club histories of the Texas League are few. The Wichita Falls Spudders are well described by Al Parker in his *Baseball Giant Killers*. The Spudders had a short thirteen-year existence 1920-32, a time when Parker was sports editor of the local newspaper. He probably saw this team more than anyone else, and the book is essentially one of reminiscence. Parker used Ruggles as his major reference and includes a number of good photographs. Do you know what a Spudder is?

The Oklahoma City 89ers published *Old Times to the Good Times--Oklahoma City Baseball*. The book covers the history of Oklahoma City through five leagues beginning in 1905. Written in the style of a sports publicist, the book summarizes the seasons of Oklahoma City baseball, most of which were spent in the Texas League. There are many pictures and reproduced newspaper headlines. Records are primarily for the American Association 89ers, through the 1980 season.

Histories of the Southern Association are limited to brief booklets on individual clubs. The best of these is *Seventy Years with The Pelicans* by Arthur Schott, the distinguished baseball historian of the state of Louisiana. This was published originally in 1957 by the New Orleans Pelicans and reissued by Mr. Schott in 1987. It is a description of baseball in New

Orleans from 1887 through the 1956 season. The performance of the club is summarized, there are brief profiles of club officials and managers and the box scores of famous games are included. An interesting feature is the opening day Pelican lineup for each season 1901-56. Highlights of the Dixie Series are included along with important club records. This is a nicely done volume which is very useful to the researcher.

League and club history is very sparse below the Double A level, consisting of short monographs for the most part. Randy Linthurst did such a work on the 1947 Trenton Giants of the Interstate League, and James Maywar wrote a brief essay on the 1926 Port Huron Saints of the Michigan-Ontario league. David Chrisman produced *The History of the Piedmont League* in 1986, that resembles closely his earlier work on the International League. Unfortunately, it has some of the same problems of inaccuracy, and its usefulness is limited. Merritt Clifton's *Disorganized Baseball*, a history of the Quebec Provincial League, is more anecdotal. *The Last Rebel Yell* by Ken Brooks gives a brief look at the Alabama-Florida League. None of these works is essential to one's library.

While it is certainly true that the amount of minor league literature is small compared to books on other subjects, the number of books is on the rise. SABR members have contributed more than their share, and there are more to come. I think we have only scratched the surface.

Bibliography

The following is a list of books referred to in this article.

Beverage, Richard E., *The Angels--Los Angeles in the Pacific Coast League 1919-1957*, Placentia, CA: The Deacon Press, 1981.

Beverage, Richard E., *The Hollywood Stars--Baseball in Movieland 1926-1957*, Placentia, CA: The Deacon Press, 1984

Bready, James H., *The Home Team*, Baltimore, 1958. Privately Published.

Brooks, Ken, *The Last Rebel Yell*, Lynn Haven, FL: Seneca Park Publishing, 1986.

Cauz, Louis, *Baseball's Back in Town*, Toronto, Controlled Media Corporation, 1977.

Chrisman, David F., *The History of the International League 1919-1960*, Pikesville, MD:, I, 1981; II, 1982; III, 1983.

Chrisman, David F., *The History of the Piedmont League*, Pikesville, MD:, 1986.

Clifton, Merritt, *Disorganized Baseball-A History of The Quebec Provincial League 1920-69*, Richford, VT: 1983.

Dolson, Frank, *Beating the Bushes*, South Bend, IN: Icarus Press, 1982.

Finch, Robert; Addington, L.H.; Morgan, Ben, *The Story of Minor League Baseball, 1901-52*, Columbus, OH: National Association, 1953.

Foster, John B., History of the National Association of Professional Baseball Leagues, Columbus, OH: National Association, 1926.

Foster, Mark S., *The Denver Bears-From Sandlots to Sellouts*, Boulder, CO: Pruett Publishing Company, 1983.

Gunther, Marc, *Basepaths*, NY: Charles Scribner's Sons, 1984.

Hampton, Bing; Petree, Patrick, *Old Times to the Good Times-Oklahoma City Baseball*, Oklahoma City 89ers, 1981.

Honig, Donald, *Up from the Minors*, NY: Cowles Book Company, 1970.

Humber, William, *Cheering for the Home Team*, Erin, Ontario, The Boston Mills Press, 1983.

Irving, Elliott, *Remembering The Vees-Richmond Virginians 1954-64*, Farmville, VA: Cumberland Printing, 1979.

Jordan, Pat, *A False Spring*, NY: Dodd Mead and Company, 1973.

Kettle, Jerry, *Low and Outside; The Confessions of a Minor Leaguer*, NY: Coward-McCann, 1965.

Lange, Fred W., *History of Baseball in California and Pacific Coast Leagues-Memories and Musings of an Old Time Baseball Player*, Oakland, CA: 1983. Privately published.

Linthurst, Randolph, *Newark Bears, Newark Bears-The Middle Years; Newark Bears-The Final Years*, West Trenton, NJ: I, 1978; II, 1979; III, 1981. Privately published.

Linthurst, Randolph, *The 1947 Trenton Giants*, West Trenton, NJ: 1982. Privately published.

LinWeber, Ralph E., *The Toledo Baseball Guide of the Mudhens*, Toledo, OH: 1944.

Mayer, Ronald A., *1937 Newark Bears-A Baseball Legend*, East Hanover, NJ: Vintage Press, 1980.

Maywar, James, *The 1926 Port Huron Saints*, Port Huron, MI: 1984. Privately published.

Nagel, Walter, *Five Straight Errors on Ladies Day*, Caldwell, ID: Caxton Press, 1965.

Obojski, Robert, *Bush League-A History of Minor League Baseball*, NY: Macmillan Publishing Company, 1975.

O'Neal, Bill, *The Texas League-A Century of Baseball 1888-1987*, Austin, TX: Eakin Press, 1987.

Overfield, Joseph M., *The 100 Seasons of Buffalo Baseball*, Kenmore, NY: Partners' Press, 1985.

Parker, Al, *Baseball Giant Killers-The Spudders of the 20s*, Quanah, TX: Nortex Press, 1976.

Remington, John L., *The Red Wings-A Love Story; A Pictorial History of Professional Baseball in Rochester, New York*, Rochester, 1969. Privately published.

Ruggles, William B., *The History of the Texas League of Professional Baseball Clubs*, Dallas, TX: Baseball League, 1932, 1951.

Ryan, Bob, *Wait Till I Make the Show*, Boston: Little, Brown and Company, 1974.

Schott, Arthur, *70 Years with the Pelicans*, New Orleans, LA: 1957.

Senzel, Howard, *Baseball and the Cold War*, NY: Harcourt, Brace, Jovanovich, 1977.

Stadler, Ken, *The Pacific Coast League-One Man's Memories 1938-57*, Los Angeles: Marbek Publications, 1984.

Tarvin, A.H., *Seventy Years on Louisville Diamonds*, Louisville, KY: Schulmann Publications, 1940.

Waddingham, Gary, *The Seattle Rainiers 1938-42*, Seattle: Writers Publishing Service, 1988.

Wolff, Rick and Pepe, Phil, *What's a Nice Harvard Boy Like You Doing in the Bushes?*, Engelwood Cliffs, NJ: Prentice Hall, 1975.

M. TIERNAN (League).

The Hurler, Rigorously Examined

By Frederick Ivor-Campbell

THE PITCHER, by John Thorn and John Holway
New York: Prentice Hall Press, 1987. $19.95

THE PITCHER BEGINS BRIL-liantly and concludes splendidly—and there is plenty of good stuff on the 272 pages in between, too. Although the book is uneven, with disappointing dips and chasms, the hillsides are pleasant, and the occasional peaks rise high enough to inspire awe.

Curiously, baseball has inspired few good poems, but Robert Francis's "Pitcher" is one of the best, and Thorn and Holway preface their book with it. Then follows a brief introduction — barely more than two pages in length, but two of the finest pages ever written about the game: a classic statement of the role of the pitcher. That the rest of the book fails to sustain the brilliance of its opening is no surprise, but if it had been executed with the care lavished on the introduction the whole book might deserve the accolade "classic."

The book proper is a melange of anecdotal and statistical analysis of the pitcher and his task, and ranges from the serious to the lighthearted, from the profound to the trivial. It reads easily: the authors have an admirable facility for lively writing. They entertain as they instruct, and if sometimes they toss in a story for its entertainment value alone—well, that's hardly a sin in baseball writing. Sometimes the authors do get carried away: chapter two, which purports to offer a psychological profile of the pitcher, turns out to be no more than a string of brief profiles of flakes. And while they almost always write clearly, once in a while they ramble off into obscurity: "He gave up one hit in the first three to open the second [inning]" (p. 228), I *think* they mean, "He gave up hits to the first three batters in the second."

This example represents what seems to me the book's principal weakness: the number of errors and mental lapses that should have been caught by critical readers before publication. In my reading I compiled a list of more than fifty such problems, ranging from the nitpicking ("less" used where "fewer" is called for), through typos (Al Spalding's "astounding won-lost mark of 255-669"), and mental lapses (asserting that the majors expanded in 1971 and that there has been "no expansion in the last fifteen years"), and careless expression (saying that Smokey Joe Williams "has never been allowed to enter the hallowed halls of Cooperstown himself" is a misleading, inflammatory way of saying he has not yet been elected to the Hall of Fame), to specious reasoning (equating surgery to repair a pitcher's arm with the use of steroids to give a weightlifter strength: "Both give the user an unfair advantage. Both are unnatural and harmful to the body.") Most worrisome, perhaps, are the obvious statistical typos. If proofreaders were unable to catch a mistake like the listing of Phil Niekro's career losses as 2 (between Eppa Rixey's 279 and Robin Roberts's 251) in a chart of big losers, how can the reader rely on the hundreds of other stats in the book?

But problems like these may not trouble the fan and general reader, who will find the book a sprightly and fascinating exploration of pitchers and their craft. Nor will they unduly trouble the serious researchers of SABR, who know enough not to rely on secondary sources anyway, who read more for the stimulus of fresh points of view and of new questions raised than for positive proofs and final answers.

Chapter One provides a suggestive and generally insightful historical survey of the development of pitching and the manipulation of pitching rules from baseball's beginnings to the present. This overview, together with the helpful appendix which shows in chart form the major changes in pitching rules and their effects on performance, provides a framework for the detailed study of the history and evolution of pitching that remains to be done.

The ten chapters that follow—on topics like control, endurance, the variety of pitches, strategy, relationships (between pitcher and coach, manager, catcher, etc.), strikeouts, wins—rely heavily on anecdotes and personality profiles (on *show* rather than *tell*) to carry the authors' argument. At its least, this approach provides fine entertainment; at its best (as in the splendid section on the beanball, pp. 38-42) it makes for a wonderfully effective communication of ideas and viewpoints.

The authors give us a nice sense of what it is to be a pitcher: how he differs from those who play other positions, how he relates to those around him, how he employs the weapons and strategies at his disposal. We come to know—albeit in a fragmentary, introductory way—many of the great (and not-so-great) pitchers of past and present. And in what might be the book's most enduring contribution, the authors try to come to grips with the measurement of pitching effectiveness—to assess pitchers' contributions to their teams' success, to establish their relative merit, to identify the truly great.

Recognizing the weakness of such traditional stats as wins and earned run average, Thorn and Holway introduce us to such recent efforts at more accurate assessment as the half-loss (which divides the blame between a pitcher who puts the losing run on base and the reliever who lets the runner score), scoring ratio (which takes into account the number of bases allowed—although this stat is not explained fully enough for the reader to grasp precisely how it is calculated), and the hold and squander for relievers who hold or squander leads. (Despite their recognition of the unreliability of pitching wins as a meaningful statistic, though, the authors devote the book's longest chapter to the win and big winners.)

In their final two chapters Thorn and Holway apply some of the new statistics to pitchers and pitching staffs. PA (pitching average) and OOBA (opponents' on base average) measure batting average and OBA from the pitcher's perspective. WAL (wins above league) records how many games a pitcher wins above the league average. And NERA (normalized earned run average) is the traditional ERA "normalized to the league average and adjusted for home-park impact." Armed with these statistics, the authors proceed to what is in some ways the highlight of the book: they choose the top pitcher for every year in each major league since 1876. To honor these pitchers they have created the Jim Creighton Award, named for one of the game's early greats. Their awards confirm the stature of pitchers like Walter Johnson, Pete Alexander and Christy Mathewson, but also spring some surprises. Dave Stieb ties Mathewson with four Creightons, and Tom Seaver surpasses him with five. Lefty Grove turns out to be the big winner, with seven Creightons, edging out Walter Johnson, who has six.

I'm uneasy with the new statistics—in part, no doubt, because some of them require for their calculation either information not readily available or a mathematician to do the work, and I don't like the feeling that my ability to understand the game is shrinking. But I also have questions about some of the stats themselves. It seems to me, for example, that some combination of on-base average and slugging percentage would mean more than PA and OOBA

(and should be little more difficult to calculate). And—as Thorn and Holway explain it, anyway—it seems to me that the NERA calculation hasn't attained a degree of sophistication sufficient to make it significantly more worthy than the plain old ERA. If we're going to have to trust the mathematicians to do our calculations, let's give them a real workout. How about factoring in the fielders' range (a hit past Larry Bowa might count less than one past Ozzie Smith) and the importance of each run (yielding a run with a ten-run lead is less damnable than giving up one that ties the game)?

Fortunately, Thorn and Holway recognize their limits ("Hey, we're human too"); their pronouncements are generally free from dogmatism, and seem offered more in the way of suggestion than demand. And if they raise more questions than they settle, that keeps us from complacency and spurs us to further examination and exploration of our own. A couple of concluding kudos. The book contains a very helpful index of names (plus a few topical entries which simply whet the appetite for more). And welcome attention is paid to pitchers from the Negro leagues (an area in which Holway is expert). One only wishes that enough statistical data were available to enable the authors to extend their Creighton awards to Negro league pitchers.

I bought The Pitcher new, at full price—something my stereotypically Scottish sensibility rarely permits. I feel the money was well spent. What stronger endorsement can you ask of a cheap Scot!

The Manly Art Analyzed

by Luke Salisbury

DISCIPLE OF A MASTER: HOW TO HIT A BASEBALL TO YOUR POTENTIAL
By Stephen J. Ferroli, Foreward by Ted Williams
Hanover, MA: Line Drive Publishing, 1987. $9.95

WHEN SABR MEMBERS assembled at St. Rita's Church for last fall's Rhode Island regional, we were surprised to see a bat sitting on a table. Such a basic tool of the game is not usually part of a research presentation. A young man in gray sweat pants and white sweat shirt got up and said he had spent his adult life studying hitting but didn't want to bore us with a technical discussion. As he talked, it was apparent Steve Ferroli had spent much of his thinking life trying to master the mysterious and difficult skill of hitting a baseball. He said anyone who wanted to discuss "mechanics" should speak to him later, and left us with two provocative remarks. Mr. Ferroli pointed out that the plate in Little League is seventeen inches wide, as it is in the big leagues, but (of course) the hitters have much shorter arms and use shorter bats. The result is strikeouts and coaches telling players to wait for a walk. "Kids standing alone at the plate and striking out is creating a generation of soccer players."

In the days before organized youth baseball, the plate was frequently a glove and kids batted until they put the ball in play. This criticism is not new, Joe Garagiola has said it many times on TV.

But then Mr. Ferroli said something not only new to us, but also to Ted Williams, whom Steve had met at baseball camp.

"When you see a baseball coming at you, you are only seeing the top half of it." Because light sources, indoor or out, are overhead, the bottom of the ball is always in shadow. Steve said as great as Williams' technique was, it could have been better if the Master had aimed for "the white," the top half of the ball. Williams had replied that he always wondered why, even with his slight upper cut, he hit as many balls on the ground as he had.

These ideas interested me enough to buy Steve's book. I'm a fan, not an athlete, and don't read instructional books, but there was such passion in Ferroli's talk of hitting, and such common sense, I thought I'd try the book.

Disciple of a Master is fascinating.

Unlike the author's modesty in front of an audience, the book starts with a jeremiad. Hitting, *Disciple* proclaims, is not all reflexes, talent, and magic. Like most human activities, it can be perfected. Ferroli reminds us that Ted Williams was 6'3", 148 pounds when he was signed and played in the minor leagues. "Where did his power come from?" Williams' and Ferroli's answer is technique. "Great hitters aren't born; they're made. They're made out of practice, fault-correction, and confidence."

Ferroli attacks the idea that averages are down in our era only because pitching is better. He says both pitchers and hitters are bigger and better athletes, but pitchers have kept pace with their art while hitters have not. The problem began in 1949 with the cutback of the minor leagues. "With teams signing fewer players...the tendency became to sign only those with exceptional ability. Professional play decided to rely on God-given talents; like foot speed, quickness, and strength...pro baseball began to invest in hitters that 'were born' not made." This caused a decline in the number of hitters who make themselves through experiment and adjustment.

Wade Boggs is a good example. Boggs won the International League batting title in 1981 hitting .335. He had hit over .300 in four of five minor league seasons but no one in the Red Sox organization was excited. Boggs couldn't run, field, or hit for power. All he had ever done was hit and all he proceeded to do was hit, but if Carney Lansford hadn't gotten hurt, Wade Boggs might never have gotten a chance.

Ted Williams is the Master *Disciple* follows. This book is a broadside in the battle between the Williams' and Charlie Lau schools of hitting. The Lau school, now taught by Red Sox' hitting coach Walt Hriniak and lauded by George Brett, holds that a hitter should hit off his front foot, hit down on the ball, and cover the entire plate, especially the outside corner. This style ideally results in line drives and singles and doubles. The Williams' style (and this harkens back to the "manly slugging/scientific hitting" debate of the 1890s — it's wonderful how little new there is under the baseball sun) holds that hitting is an act into which one must put *all* the body's resources. Williams spoke of "cocking the hips" and Ferroli takes this farther by breaking hip action into "pre-swing" and "stretch position." The key to hitting is that the lower body moves forward as the upper body moves back, and then both go forward. There is a very specific way to do this. The purpose of the "stretch position" is to get the body moving before the pitcher releases the ball. This increases the time the hitter has to decide to swing by half a second. I actually tried this with a bat I've had since I fantasized I was Harvey Kuenn winning the batting title, and the "stretch position" does seem to make my swing quicker.

Disciple tells you everything you could possibly want to know about swinging a bat, and probably a little more too. There's "landing and hip rotation," "movements of the arms," where the elbows should be, "pre-extension," "the path of the hands," proper knuckle alignment, grip, position of the bottom arm, stride movement, bending the back leg, follow through, everything. An entire chapter is devoted to whether a hitter should upper-cut. Another chapter dissects the strike zone. Other chapters describe "other strokes" like the "inside out" swing or proscribe practice routines. The last critiques books by Rod Carew and Pete Rose.

The "manly slugging/scientific hitting" - Lau/Williams split is one of those basic differences that mirror ways of looking at life. Do you react defensively, minimize risk, and be consistent but not spectacular? Or do you "go for it," try to get the most out of yourself, and make the world bend to your will? At the plate every man has his choice and Steve Ferroli believes hitting should be done full throttle. He recommends a hitter stop guessing with two strikes and shorten his stroke but believes everyone would be a better hitter if he hit full body for two strikes. Ferroli thinks Carew might have hit .425 if he hadn't been a defensive hitter and Pete Rose could have had a higher average and hit home runs. He also thinks George Brett says he hits Lau-style but actually switches to Williams' during his swing.

Disciple of a Master does for hitting what Bill James did for statistics. It approaches old problems and old ways of thinking with logic and common sense. Too many of us have relegated the complex act of hitting a baseball to the realm of mystery when it is an art that demands analysis.

The Master Speaks
by Jim L. Sumner

MY TURN AT BAT
By Ted Williams and John Underwood
New York: Fireside Books (Simon & Schuster), 1988. $7.95

IT'S BEEN ALMOST THREE decades since Ted Williams' dramatic career-ending home run at Fenway Park. If anything, his reputation as one of the premier hitters in baseball history has increased during the ensuing years. In particular the unsuccessful attempts of Rod Carew, George Brett, Wade Boggs and others to climb the .400 peak last scaled by Williams in 1941 have expanded his legend. Evidence of the continued interest in the Splendid Splinter is the reissue, with some expansion, of *My Turn at Bat*, his 1969 "autobiography" written with John Underwood.

Although not a pathbreaking masterpiece by any means *My Turn at Bat* easily avoids the bland whitewash characteristic of all too many sports autobiographies. Williams was a controversial player and he does not hesitate to elaborate on virtually every aspect of that controversy. He is particularly forthcoming concerning his frequently acrimonious relationship with the Boston press. In fact the alleged abuses of numerous Boston newsmen are an ongoing theme in the book. Williams also discusses his unhappy home life, difficulties with his draft board, periodic bouts of fan booing, his refusal to tip his hat, the "Boudreau shift," his matrimonial failures, and his predilection for hunting and fishing, among other areas of interest.

Fortunately not all of the book is in this negative vein. The positive aspects of Williams come through clearly: his attention to detail, his work habits, his fierce pride and competitiveness. Although the expected discussions of the fine points of hitting are interspersed throughout the book, Williams also goes to some length to defend his skills as a fielder, baserunner, and team player.

Underwood is notably unobtrusive in his role of collaborator. *My Turn at Bat* is conversational and anecdotal, with only a loose chronological framework. What it loses in structural complexity, however, it makes up for in immediacy and readability. A reader can easily imagine Williams is in his living room, discussing the fine points of analyzing an pitcher or tying flies.

There are some additions to the original 1969 edition. The most interesting of these is the concluding section, an ambivalent discussion of Williams' up and down career as a manager. Current observations on such subjects as the possiblity of a Boggs or Mattingly batting .400, the DH, and artificial turf are blended into the text. The new material doesn't appreciably change the focus or scope of the Williams saga but does bring it up to date.

There is certainly a definitive Ted Williams biography waiting to be written. Even when it is written, however, *My Turn at Bat* will remain must reading for fans of Williams, the Red Sox, and baseball. Its reavailability, at a reasonable price, is to be welcomed.

A Lively History, Classroom or No

By Joseph Overfield

BASEBALL FROM A DIFFERENT ANGLE
By Bob Broeg and William J. Miller, Jr.
South Bend, IN: Diamond Communications, 1988. $12.95

DIAMOND COMMUNICA-tions, which gave us *The Roaring Redhead* and *Voices of the Game*, has undertaken another major baseball project with *Baseball From A Different Angle*, co-authored by Bob Broeg, long-time columnist and sports editor of the St. Louis Post-Dispatch and prolific writer on baseball subjects, and William J. Miller, Jr., a St. Louis University history professor. It is the understanding of this reviewer, who, incidentally, worked with the galley proofs and not the final product, that it was Professor Miller who did the research and Broeg who did the writing. Also cited as contributors are two other St. Louisans, writer Dan Krueckeberg and ball park expert Carl Schoen. The aim of the authors, as stated in the introduction, was to write a text book for Professor Miller's classes and for sports history courses at other campuses, with the hope it might also have trade-book possibilities.

If you buy this book, and this is not meant as a rap, do not expect to get Harold Seymour or David Q. Voigt. What you will get is a delightful mixture of baseball history, humor and opinion, uniquely conceived and well presented. You will not find a footnote and, regretfully, there is no index. The writing, as one would expect from Broeg, is sprightly, informal (Frank Robinson is "F. Robby" and Brooks Robinson is "B. Robby") and anecdotal, wherein lies its greatest charm.

What is unique about this Broeg-Miller book? For one thing, it is really 14 different books in one, with each chapter capable of standing on its own, which is probably ideal for classroom use. The concept was to take 14 important aspects and of the game and tell each one's story from alpha to omega. Since most of the subjects have already had whole books written about them, the authors' task was a formidable one. They have pulled it off smartly, within reasonable limits of space, with room left for numerous lively digressions. For example, in a discussion of "soaking" in the game's primeval days, we learn that Pepper Martin, "The Wild Horse of the Osage," never wore sanitary socks; and in the chapter on relief pitching there is a side trip to acquaint the reader with the alcoholic peccadilloes of Bugs Raymond, who was not a relief pitcher.

Among the subjects dealt with (each with a clever title) are the baseball ("Spheres of Influence,") mitts and uniforms, ball parks, the rules and their evolution, movement of franchises, umpires, scandals, playing managers, writers, radio men, relief pitchers and salaries. The 14th and final chapter, "What Cy Saw," artfully surveys and evaluates the changes in baseball over the lifetime of Cy Young (1867-1955).

While the book is not numbers oriented, enough statistics are used to satisfy those who devour that sort of thing. Stats are used most effectively to demonstrate how changes in the ball have influenced the record book and individual careers. The same tactic is used in the discussion of ball parks ("Of Real Estate and Unreal Hitters.") An interesting point is made in connection with Sportsmans' Park, St. Louis. In 1930 the Browns had a 30-foot screen erected in left field. In 1932, when Jimmy Foxx hit 58 home runs, he supposedly hit 12 balls off that screen, although some accounts say it was seven. Whether it was 12, seven or even three, the fact remains that had the screen not been there baseball history would have been changed and it would have been Double-X and not The Babe whom Roger Maris chased in 1961.

The difficult subject of baseball scandals is particularly well handled. A nice touch is the follow-ups on what happened to the eight Black Soxers after they were barred. The alleged game-throwing incident involving Ty Cobb and Tris Speaker is dealt with in detail. Interestingly, the authors suggest that had Judge Landis ruled against the two super stars (and he might well have

done so, had Dutch Leonard, the accuser, come to Chicago to testify in person) baseball might have been so rocked there would have been no Hall of Fame. This is possible, of course, but it should be remembered that the game did survive and the Hall of Fame was born, notwithstanding the defections of Hal Chase, Buck Weaver, Joe Jackson and the others. As to the book's treatment of the Black Sox scandal, it is the view here that too much of the blame is attributed to the penury of White Sox owner Charles Comiskey, and not enough to the perfidy of Chick Gandil and the human frailty and avarice of the others. After all, there were thousands of woefully underpaid bank tellers at that time who did not rob their banks, and hundreds of woefully underpaid ballplayers who did not throw games.

Special mention should be made of the chapters on writers ("Press Box Poets and Pests") and broadcasters ("The Eyes of the Fan.") Author Broeg's lifetime in the press box fits him uniquely to tell these stories, which he does with authority and humor.

I said the book is anecdotal, and I was not (in the words of one of Bob Broeg's favorite characters, Dizzy Dean) "just whistlin' Dixie." A favorite concerns J.G. Taylor Spink, flamboyant publisher of *The Sporting News*, and tiny Miller Huggins. After Spink intervened for Huggins, who was trying to become manager of the Yankees, he sent the little guy off to New York with this warning: "Crissakes, don't wear that damn cap. Jake Ruppert already thinks you're a jockey." Once, the old-time outfielder, Jesse Burkett, then baseball coach at Holy Cross, was asked for a scouting report on a young catcher named Leo Hartnett. Said Burkett: "He'll never make it to the big leagues, his hands are too small."

Also good for a chuckle is the story of how author Broeg shamed Gussie Busch into making Stan Musial the National League's first $100,000 man. And then, when Bob Feller was in his youthful prime, no pitcher was more intimidating. On October 2, 1938, the last day of the season, Feller struck out 18, and nobody was digging in. Outfielder Chet Laabs, who was of Polish descent and who fanned five times, summed it up best: "Why die so young when the beer is cold and the kielbassa hot?"

When Bob Broeg comments on sports writing, it behooves us all to listen. He maintains there is far too much "jockstrap sniffing" among modern reporters, who, after their mad post-game rushes to the clubhouse, usually come up with such gems as "He hit a high slider." What is wrong, he asks, with a good narrative account of the game? To which I add, amen!

Mr. Broeg never saw an alliteration he didn't like. Rogers Hornsby is "a tough talking Texan," Phil Ball, redundantly, perhaps, is "a curt curmudgeon;" Mr. Spink of *The Sporting News* "the terrible tempered Taylor," and Bill Veeck "the colorful, collarless character." With Bob, it is the "bashful Browns" and the "phutile Phillies," while the Athletics "languish in lower latitudes." On some old-time writers: They were. "purple-prosed-and-poetic-put-'em-on-pedestal...." His description of underpaid ballplayers - "the poorest peons in polyester" — must put him right up there in the Alliteration Hall of Fame, along with Spiro Agnew's (courtesy of Pat Buchanan) "nattering nabobs of negativism." Not an alliteration, but typically Broeg is his description of Ray Blades: "razor sharp," naturally.

Baseball From A Different Angle is factual but never dull; it is light in style but heavy in its grasp of baseball history. Those who use it in the classroom, or outside, are in for a treat.

Fun in the Sun
by Eliot Cohen

THE BASEBALL FAN'S GUIDE TO SPRING TRAINING
By Mike Shatzkin and Jim Charlton
Reading, MA: Addison-Wesley, $9.95. 288 pp. (paper)

GRAPEFRUIT LEAGUE ROAD TRIP
By Ken Coleman and Dan Valenti
Lexington, MA: The Stephen Greene Press, $7.95. 164 pp. (paper)

ONE OF THE BEAUTIES OF traveling to spring training is that you don't need a book to tell you how to do it. A healthy appetite for baseball, wheels, and an appropriate state road map will pull you through. *The Baseball Fan's Guide to Spring Training* and *Grapefruit League Road Trip*, issued for spring training '88, both offer limited assistance and trip enrichments, while omitting certain essentials that can enable the first-time traveller to avoid rookie mistakes.

Road Trip is basically a travel guide to Florida camps, laying out how to get to the games and what else to do in the area. Straightforward information on ballpark ambiance, local attractions and restaurants is broken up with swatches of spring color. There are classic spring antics retold, discussions of citrus circuit economics, and quotes from players and others--such as broadcaster/co-author Ken Coleman--on the charms of the pre-season. This book beat its rival to the stores, at the cost of placing the Reds in Tampa, rather than their new Plant City camp, 20 miles to the west.

The *Guide* is more of a baseball book which gives it value for readers who make their closest contact with the citrus league via a juice glass. The book opens with a light history of the growth and development of spring training, touching on the famous names and spiced with period photos. Team essays recap top spring prospects during the last three decades, many of whom showed the staying power of footprints in the sand.

For their travel tips, authors Jim Charlton and Mike Shatzkin divide the teams into geographical groups, three for Florida, one for Arizona, with regional introductions giving driving distance charts, area attractions, airports, and radio stations that carry local games. Team sections point out the almost uniform worthlessness of "team hotels" (no one stays there except the team physician) and list players' favorite leisure spots, but advise checking with the chamber of commerce or travel agents for specifics on the towns themselves. Noting that Shatzkin is a founder of Sunball, which operates tours to the Florida camps, readers will find this dearth of information either surprising or predictable, depending on their level of faith in mankind.

Either book will help the neophyte find the parks, although the same information is available in local newspaper supplements found in nearly every circuit paper on or about the third Sunday of February. The Miami *Herald* offers the best of the bunch, with previews, directions, maps and phone numbers for the grapefuit league clubs, plus spring rosters for all 26 teams.

Both books pound on the relaxed atmosphere and greater accessibility of players, but fail to touch on several critical questions about making the spring training trek. Neither book offers a clue as to budgets. Florida's department of commerce estimates that the out-of-state grapefruit league visitor spends an average of $164 per day, $1150 total plus air fare. My experience says that the staggering Florida figure can be reduced by two-thirds or more.

Spring training can be made affordable if you book your rental cars and lodgings in advance at the best rates. Keep in mind that motel rates vary wildly, even within a couple of blocks. There are plenty of $70 a night rooms out there, but good ones for $30 and under as well. Florida has become the world capital of the salad bar and its offspring, which includes pasta, tacos, soups and desserts, eliminating the need to exceed a $5 dinner bill unless you really want gourmet cuisine. One place you won't save money is at the ballpark, where ticket and concession stand prices hover near major league levels.

The books exalt the joys of attending practices prior to the opening of the exhibition season. Attending a day of practice gives fans a behind-the-scenes look at the game, but one three-hour session will be enough for anyone not researching coaching techniques. Depending on site, you may be able to wander to other fields. (A *Guide* tip for games applies here, too--always walk completely around the park, or practice complex, before settling down. While you're watching Alfredo Griffin take BP, Sandy Koufax might be teaching the curve ball on another diamond.) But at some facilities, you'll be restricted to a single diamond and see enough 3-1 drills to last a lifetime. Intrasquad games are much more fun. At the Expos intrasquad opener, Casey Candaele tried a back flip--he looked like a sack of laundry falling over--taking the field and Hubie Brooks attempted a snatch catch on his first flyball. With the team split in two, some regulars played longer than they would during the first two weeks' games and about ten different pitchers got some work.

Both books advocate establishing a base from which you'll fan out to cover the teams within a region. That idea succeeds if you're concentrating on a single favorite club. For multi-club interests, the theory works in Arizona for the first two weeks of the exhibition, when six teams play daily in the greater Phoenix area, and in central Florida, but it's difficult on the Florida coasts. Particularly in the Dunedin to Sarasota corridor, coastal traffic is abysmal. Greg Gross of the Phillies doesn't complain about the bus trips, but about "bus sits" on Route 19, a boulevard perpetually under construction and choked with cars which pretends to connect Clearwater to the outside world. The 24 miles from downtown St. Petersburg to Dunedin is at least an hour's drive during normal hours.

For travel guides, both books conspicuously lack inside information. They scream for a "best bets" section on the areas that would tell you about the best smorgasbord in town, some spectacular $32.50 per night motel, the top roadside citrus stands, or a particular country road that reminds travellers that Florida is more than Quik-Stop gas/food combos. Except for painstaking descriptions of the ballpark ambiance, which after a time become repetitive, little in these books conveys a sense of the unique charms and pitfalls of a given community.

For example, Sarasota's Payne Park (which passed into oblivion after this spring's schedule) has no legal parking nearby, except on Sundays, when the meters are not read at an adjacent municipal lot, so that's the best day to attend if you have a choice. Sarasota is also the toughest place to find a motel vacancy and one of the priciest, so plan

that segment. Kissimmee's Disney strip, on the other hand, is wide open, with great rates, so shop around. Remember though, that the Astros' park is about the same distance from Tinker Field in Orlando as the Magic Kingdom. The University of Miami, a perennial collegiate powerhouse, plays almost all of its March schedule at home, at night during the week, usually entertaining ranked northern teams escaping the cold. Neither book suggests that side trip over the Parrot Jungle.

The books help the prospective traveller by emphasizing the need to buy most tickets in advance as spring training is fast becoming a victim of its own success, setting annual attendance records throughout the '80s. It's not yet a case of nobody-goes-there-because-it's-too-crowded, but fans may find themselves shut out of some teams' games without advance planning. But overall, spring training remains an informal, impromptu experience, and the ABCs of a successful trip needn't include either of these books.

"TEN THOUSAND EYES WERE ON HIM AS HE RUBBED HIS HANDS WITH DIRT"

"BUT THERE IS NO JOY IN MUDVILLE — MIGHTY CASEY HAS STRUCK OUT"

"WHENEVER HOPPER APPEARS BEFORE THE FOOTLIGHTS"

A Great Writer, Essentially a Fan

by Bill Borst

SEASON TICKET: A BASEBALL COMPANION
By Roger Angell
Boston: Houghton Mifflin, 1988. $18.95

WITHOUT FAIL, EVERY spring the baseball-reading public can count on a plethora of baseball books that inform us as to how severe Lenny Dykstra's jockitch is, or what incredibly funny things happened to Tim McCarver behind the mike. Every five years, Roger Angell publishes a book that quickly reminds the baseball fan what the game is really about. The latest in his quinquennial look at America's game, *Season Ticket*, seriously rivals *Summer Game*, the initial book, in his quadrilogy, spanning some twenty years of writing. To paraphrase Red Barber, after a long and baseball-less winter, *Season Ticket* is "just what the doctor ordered."

Kevin Horrigan of the St. Louis *Post-Dispatch* calls Angell "an artist with a press credentials." He is *not* a baseball writer, or in the parlance of of the press box, he is not a "ballwriter!" He is essentially an exceptional writer, who prefers spending his time observing, thinking and musing about baseball. Roger Angell is a baseball fan. His lyrical pursuit of the essence of not only the "game between the lines," but also

people behind the scenes is central to his success as a writer. He is keenly aware that "the game can break your heart! No other sport elucidates failures so plainly, or presents itself in such painful and unexpected variety."

Whatever the conversation, whatever the topic, Roger Angell studies the game from the fan's perspective and asks penetrating questions of the professionals, the people who can best answer the questions that the denizens of the grandstand would like to know but seldom get the opportunity to ask.

All of this is evidence of Angell's dichotomous nature. With reference to baseball's drug and periodic salary disputes, the journalist in him tried to report objectively the issues as they related to the game, but the fan, the more dominant of his bifurcated personality, was angry, as if caught in a malaise that afflicted him in a "fungoid fashion" every time he realized the inevitable clash between baseball "as I wanted it to be and baseball as it unescapably and unhappily seems to be."

Like a modern day Odysseus, Angell checks the schedule and follows where his heart leads him around his baseball world, whether it be the casual atmosphere of spring training in Arizona or Florida, or the more serious and competitive ball yards of Baltimore and Busch Stadium. Angell is a twentieth century version of Bunyan's "Everyfan," an eager pilgrim in search of baseball's eternal verities.

The author is a purist who believes that baseball is best enjoyed and understood at the ball park. He underscores his belief that "baseball can't really be taken in on television because of our ingrained habits of TV-watching. Anyone who knows the sport, knows that the ninth inning is as valid as the first inning — that's why real fans stay to the end of a game. But we don't watch TV that way. ...On TV the primary emphasis is the score and the possibility of the other team's changing it...and so we miss the integrity of the nine innings and those multiples of three — three strikes and three outs. People can't learn to watch baseball that way; they're just learning to watch television."

Angell's books read like scrapbooks, as his word pictures take the reader back to a frozen moment in the writer's life. Reading Angell is akin to re-reading old newspaper accounts that have, as if magically, taken on a new form that somehow transcends time, place and score.

The author is at his literary best when discussing pitching, the most scientific aspect of baseball, unless Ted Williams is on the other end of the conversation and the subject is hitting. Whether it be with the inimitable "Quis," Dan Quisenberry, the flaky relief specialist of the Kansas City Royals, or Giants' manager Roger Craig elucidating his split-fingered fastball, or merely kibitzing with such diverse students of the mound as Warren Spahn, Syd Thrift of the Pirates, or Charlie Leibrandt of the Royals, Angell demonstrates a perceptibility that always seems to be on the mark. His "thinking out loud" about what the DH may be doing to the fragile pitching arms of American League hurlers is quite interesting, if not provocative. Angell correctly perceived that three Cy Young winners in a row were subsequently disabled and forced from the game, namely Steve Stone, Rollie Fingers and Pete Vuckovich.

As good a questioner as he is, Angell is an even better listener, perhaps the real secret to his love affair with baseball. He does what you and I would love to do, sit down and quiz the masters of the game on virtually every little secret, every fine point of this complex game, all the time, listening intently as players and coaches reveal their innermost thoughts. Angell lauds Earl Weaver for his mastery of the post-game interview, or his "postgame seminars." "I expect to walk into Weaver's office one night and find waiting ushers, with programs and flashlights..."

When Angell is personally involved, as he was during the 1986 World Series, the "penultimate series," when, not just one, but both of his teams were playing, he is truly at his enthusiastic best. As he wrote "No poll or instrument can determine whether such paroxysms of fan feeling were felt in more distant parts, away from the big-city narcissism of Mets-mania or from the peat fires of devotion and doubt of the Red Sox faithful, but it is my guess that every fan was affected by these to some degree."

Season Ticket is not without humor. Angell notes in a moment of profound whimsy that of the San Diego pitching staff in the 1984 World Series, three were card-carrying members of the John Birch Society. Angell struggled to find some sort of pattern here. "Two were starters and one a reliever. . .two were left-handed and one of those, Dave Dravecky, (now of the Giants), hit right-handed." With the calculated response of a master rhetorician, Angell left it up to "that demon Sabermetrician," Bill James, to "devise the first Birchfactor formula and thereby return our game to the pure world of numbers, where it belongs." One can just imagine Angell's tongue nearly protruding through his cheek.

Cardinal fans might enjoy Angell's vivid description of what has now become a Cardinal tradition in the eighties: the rite of watching the gates fling open at Busch Stadium and the Clydesdales trot onto the Astroturf, pulling behind them a "shining beer wagon, stacked high with cartons of Bud," and on the top next to "a waggy Dalmatian" the patriarch of the Busch empire, August Busch Jr., the "diminutive 86-year old millionaire-owner-brewer, bravely waving his plumed Cardinal-red chapeau as he hangs on for dear life. . ." One can only wonder what the author's views on Spuds McKenzie might be.

With a wit that could rival that of Johnny Carson, Angell muses aloud, "I wondered if this precedent might encourage Mr. Steinbrenner to cruise the Yankee Stadium outfield in a replica tanker."

He verbally captures so many of the game's marvelous moments, such as the heroic effort of catcher Buck Martinez of the Toronto Blue Jays in a game against the Seattle Mariners, suffering a broken leg and a dislocated ankle in a collision at the plate, in which the runner was out. In severe pain Martinez's mind struggled to keep his broken body in the continuing play, as he inadvertently threw the ball into the outfield in a vain attempt to get the other runner going to third. This runner, Gorman Thomas, became the next out, as Martinez fielded the toss, and tagged him out at the plate in a valiant double play. If you are keeping score it went 8-2-7-2.

Season Ticket, as are all of the author's books, is deeply rooted in history. If Angell is writing about relief pitchers, then a history of how that specialty developed becomes part of his presentation. Everything is against his vast backdrop of the past, whether it be watching Pete Rose with the specter of Ty Cobb playing alongside, or writing about baseball and drugs and the obvious comparisons with the 1919 betting scandal.

In a chapter that might best be described as "baseball whimsy," Angell writes about baseball luck and what he calls "fortuity." "These accidental events are important because you always have to make some response to them." In talking with Sandy Alderson outside the A's locker room, it is always something. "Injuries, bad hops, bad calls. . .teams must rise above them." For Roger Angell the fan, "everything is beyond my control. . .every part of the game is just fortuity." In a moment of personal reflection the author provides us with his insight. "We want our teams to be losers as well as winners;

we must have bad luck as well as good luck, terrible defeats and disappointments, as well as victories, and thrilling surprises." He adds that "losing, rather than winning, is what baseball is all about and that's why it is a game for adults."

Many would disagree with this idea, but the author suggests that anything else and "we would lose baseball." Perhaps his pessimism, which here borders on masochism is inherent from rooting for the Red Sox for so long.

It is fitting and just that his book end with a trip to Cooperstown, that baseball shrine that enables the fan to remove himeself from the noise and the confusion of a grueling pennant race, and like some weary pilgrim, pause for a moment's reflection in what is baseball's answer to the chapels of Lourdes or St. Peter's Basilica.

As the author so poignantly points out, "the artifacts and the exhibits in the Hall remind us vividly and with feeling, of our hopes for our bygone seasons and teams and players. Memories are jogged even jolted, colors become brighter and we laugh or sigh, remembering good times gone by." As long as Roger Angell is around to chronicle and jolt our memories, these times will be continually relived, truly sustaining "the elegance of our baseball dreams."

Season Ticket is not a book for everyone. Some casual fans, or those without any sense of baseball history or appreciation for literary work, would probably be more at ease reading something like *Rocket Man* or *Bats*. Angell's book is for the serious student of the game, who should be prepared to devote several hours not only reading it but savoring it as well. I am certain that the sixteenth century essayist, Sir Francis Bacon had books of this magnitude in mind when in his *Of Studies*, he wrote ". . . some few are to be chewed and digested . . . and some few are to be read wholly, and with diligence and attention."

The author modestly says that "anyone can explain baseball." That may be so but too few can do it with his perception and his literary flair. Roger Angell puts baseball on its highest intellectual level, harvesting what is fruit for scholar and nectar for the pure fan. He says "we fans never quite learn this game, but there are rewards in trying." Well, there are many rewards in reading about baseball, especially when Roger Angell is the author. With the possible exception of Tom Boswell, no writer has ever captured on paper what "our passionate preoccupation with this complex sturdy and elegant game" really means.

A Conversation with Roger Angell

by Dick Johnson

Roger Angell's office at The New Yorker, *where he works as senior fiction editor and baseball reporter, has the rumpled busy look of a college professor's study. Shelves are lined with baseball guides, SABR publications, autographed baseballs, odd wire sculptures of ballplayers and framed photos of a stern Bob Gibson and smiling Garrison Keillor and others. Of special interest were a photo of Yaz leaning heavily against the Green Monster talking, no doubt, to the scoreboard boy, and a hand colored engraving of Bill Campbell in pitching sequence, looking like an antique military manual of arms.*

I talked with Roger Angell on a gray Friday afternoon in late winter, days before the start of spring training. He poured me a cup of coffee as we began our conversation.

Q. Describe your background as a fan.

A. I grew up in New York as a Yankee and Giant fan, not the Dodgers. They were distant and not very good. I was a big Giant fan, especially for Carl Hubbell and, with the Yankees, for Joe DiMaggio.

My father had put me onto baseball. He had grown up in Cleveland and had been a big Indians fan all his life. I shifted my own loyalties to the Red Sox in the fifties. Being a Yankee fan wasn't much fun because they won all the time. I spent a lot of time in New England. I went to Harvard, and I had a New England family and saw a lot of Red Sox suffering down east in Maine.

Q. Did you ever aspire to be a sportswriter?

A. I never wanted to be a baseball writer, but I wanted to be a writer. I wrote for more than twenty years - stories, articles, books. Becoming a baseball writer occurred a great deal later, although in many ways I think I am not a baseball writer at all. I've never been a beat writer and those are the guys who really know the game. I do something different, not necessarily something better. I admire them and I feel that being fresh, day to day, and continuing relationships with and against players and so forth, is the highest form of baseball journalism.

Q. How do you select the topics and personalities about which you write?

A. I think that the people I've chosen are for evident reasons. I did a piece on Dan Quisenberry because he was so unusual in his character and personality, and because relief pitching is such a special part of the game. He is wonderfully articulate and intelligent.

I did Bob Gibson because he was just plain fearsome. I realized I was scared of him even after he had left the game, but he was an amazing interview -- absolutely open and honest.

I find that I do mention many of the same people in my baseball pieces, year after year. My list of baseball friends and acquaintances is growing, but it's most useful to go to people who are knowledgeable and sound about the game, and who feel confident talking to me. Bill Rigney, for instance. He's been in baseball all his life, he has a great memory, and a lovely feeling for the game. He's funny, too. He's great company.

I am still learning baseball, thank God, and I expect I always will be. I find the best people in the game are always the ones who tell me that they are still learning, too.

Q. Who are some of your baseball friends?

A. Well, Peter Gammons is one of them. I talk baseball with him both to find out what's going on in the game and to share our passion for it. We often sit together at games. It's a funny thing -- if we've been together at a playoff game or a Series game, I will find observations and ideas of his in my writing later on, and I've noticed that some of my observations and ideas creep into *his* pieces. This is fine, I think; we're friends, and we trust and admire each other. I know I get more from this than he does, because Peter is more in the game than anyone I know. He was a wonderful newspaper writer, back with the Boston *Globe*; his output was extraordinary.

Ron Fimrite, of *Sports Illustrated*, is also a close friend. Dave Bush, with the San Francisco *Chronicle*, is a great baseball friend who will talk long distance for hours. I have friends in New York whom I consider invaluable. There's the writer Peter Schjeldahl, a poet and art critic. He and his wife are passionate Mets fans. When I wrote about what Mets fans were doing in 1986 they were among those I profiled. There is a poet colleague of mine here at *The New Yorker* named Alistair Reid, who tells me about baseball in the Dominican Republic, where he lives.

Your question in a larger sense is about baseball as a form of belonging, a form of having friends, a community. It's a wonderful thing when a team wins for the first time and the fans discover each other. Whole groups of people begin to realize that there are people all around them who have been suffering in the same way over the years and have the same memories of bygone players and teams. This was very evident during last year with the Twins, and I tried to write about that.

I am fortunate because I get a steady flow of baseball mail, letters from people I don't know. Some of them have become pen pals and even private stringers. They write me about baseball in Seattle and San Diego, but mostly they write about themselves. I think that it's not stretching a point to say that baseball has filled in for quite some significant areas of life that mean less to us than they once did: our politics, our cities, our families, and our sense of community. I think all these connections are somewhat crumbled in our society while baseball feels very much the same as it always did, at least in the sense that we belong to the game in the same way. It is therapeutic and exciting to have this conversation, which can be conducted almost on a national basis. The other side of this, of which I have written, is the bitterness that you sometimes sense, among the dedicated non-fans — that edge of scorn in a look or a bitter joke which contains a good deal of envy. I think that people who don't belong to baseball see how much it means to us in a serious sense, and they envy that.

Q. What factors do you think have contributed to the rise in both the quantity and quality of baseball writing?

A. Well, I thought all along that baseball was different from other sports, and that some of its special qualities were conducive to good writing. When my first book, *The Summer Game*, came out in 1972, I went around the country on publicity tours, and most of the TV and radio people I encountered seemed amused and a little scornful that anyone would still want to write about baseball. They felt baseball was all finished, that it was a game watched by old folks and kids. Pro football was very much the king of sports back then.

I don't feel that way. Baseball is not like our other sports. It uses time in a different way, so it's difficult to encompass and program on television. We watch too many sporting events on television, I'm afraid. Every weekend, almost every day, there's an inundation of "championship" events. I think fans have become surfeited with this, and they've begun to notice that since baseball is slower, and that it's played day by day, all through its season, it is pleasing to us in quite another way. Fans and writers have seemed to come to this realization at the same time. Baseball is the perfect writer's sport: it's linear, there's time to take notes, make drawings, and think idle thoughts. In my case, which is probably different from other writers, because of the space I am given, baseball is also a way of writing about myself.

I think, too, a lot of writers who were not sportswriters began to sense that baseball was a way to spread themselves a little bit. It's very inviting for literary people to seem manly and at home in the world of sports, and all. It's inviting to be writing about the American Game. Writers want to connect themselves to their childhood and there are easy connections there — to childhood, to fathers and sons, and to the evocations of a simpler past. These things seem very obvious to me.

Of course the deepest lure of any sport may be that it provides us with heroes -- people to whom something has happened that's more difficult than what is happening to us on a given day. We can see them dealing with it or *not* dealing with it, and both alternatives are seductive to us. This is always visible in baseball, which is both a team game and an individual game, where individuals stand out.

Q. Who would you say are some of the best current baseball authors?

A. Well, there are a lot of them, but I try not to answer this question because I invariably leave someone out.

Let me answer this another way and mention some of my all time favorite baseball books. I would start with Lawrence Ritter's *The Glory of Their Times*, a classic work that opened up the past of baseball for us all. The second edition is also a great and important book, with its wonderful chapter on Hank Greenberg.

Q. What of baseball fiction? I have a friend who theorizes that baseball fiction is so hard to pull off because real baseball is so much better.

A. I wrote that years ago. I find it hard to get involved with it. It's so hard to create a whole world that could equal what we know about this particular day in the majors. But I thought the first two novels by Mark Harris were excellent. They were something that hadn't been done before. They were rich and inventive and funny.

Q. Would you say that Ring Lardner was the first baseball novelist with You Know Me, Al?

A. I enjoyed it but I haven't read it for years. Those days were so different. He was really writing humor about hicks and rubes, when ballplayers were guys with straw suitcases. A lot of the humor in that book is about people not knowing their way around. This isn't true anymore. Ballplayers catch up very quickly, even if they have come from, say, a backwater in Latin America; after one swing through the league they become dazzling cosmopolitans.

I can remember the players I encountered 25-30 years ago when I first began doing this and I'm certain there is a higher level of education and sophistication, an awareness of the media, and so forth, with today's player. I also think that the players' understanding of baseball is a lot better. They have been much better coached and many of them have a greater understanding and appreciation of the game.

Q. Have you found any players that are particularly literary?

A. There are some, but I don't want to talk about that because it would sound as if I'm saying the other players are dumb. Sure, I've met players who talk about books, who read.

Let me say this another way. There are guys in the game who talk wonderfully about baseball and I go to them again and again, because as a reporter I'd be stupid not to. Also, I learn. When I did the long piece about catching for my new book I had the impression that catchers knew enormous amounts about baseball. They seemed further into the game than other players. They were a wonderful group to talk with. Most of what catchers do is overlooked and they love to talk about what they do, and their relationship with pitchers, umpires, hitters. The whole game is in front of them. Among them you find people like Ted Simmons, Bob Boone (a brilliant conversationalist about baseball), and Carlton Fisk. As a reporter in any field you would always go back to the best talkers.

This brings up another subject that has always interested me -- the fact that the most interesting players to talk to are usually the older players. They have all gone through the process of changing from young stars, who didn't really understand how the game was played because of their enormous inherent talent. When those skills begin to leave them they have to learn the responses and actions they have been using by instinct, and that's when they begin to think about the game. At that point some of them become fans for the first time. There are a lot of ballplayers out there who play the game wonderfully but don't really care. It's just another sport to them, because they were also great football and basketball players and chose baseball.

I did a piece about hitting in *Late Innings*, and in it I mentioned older players who told me that they wished they had known as much about hitting when they were beginning as they had learned at the end of their careers. Others said that just at the time they learned the game they had to leave it. That's interesting, and you can usually get a veteran's attention when you discuss the intricacies of baseball. Younger players aren't that involved.

Q. What elements of the game do you miss that were there when you first started to write about the game?

A. I miss daytime ball, now a rarity, and daytime World Series games, a terrible loss. I miss some of the old ballparks. More will be gone soon. Tiger Stadium is probably going to go, Comiskey Park, too. I miss grass. Grass is still infinitely preferable than artificial turf. I miss that play behind second base where the shortstop can *just* get to a ball with the last half inch of his grasp and pick up a slow bouncer and throw out the runner at first. That's a beautiful play that's just about gone on an artificial surface.

I've written about what we've lost and what we're losing but I don't think about baseball with a catch in my throat. I don't have sentimental thoughts about the grand old game. I resent some of the changes, I am wary of others that I think are going to come, but so far the game is played just about the way it always has been.

Q. Which baseball figures of the past would you have wanted to meet and write about?

A. Just the obvious ones. I don't think I have any great insights on players of the past that most fans don't already share. I would have loved to have seen Cobb play; I saw Ruth quite a bit; I also would have enjoyed seeing Walter Johnson, and Christy Mathewson. But I don't think about the baseball past that much. I think that the absence of a dominant team is something that some fans miss a lot. I can't decide if this is a good thing or a bad thing. We haven't had a repeater in the playoffs in this decade or a repeater in the Series since the seventies. It's always fun to have a dominant team during a decade and see other people try to knock it off.

The seventies had the Oakland A's and the Cincinnati Reds as the two great teams of that decade, with the Yankees not quite reaching that level at the end. I think that older fans look back to the old Yankees with longing and I'm not so sure that's justified. The Yankees so dominated baseball that we thought of them in the same terms as imperial Rome. But the way they won was by beating up on teams in the second division. I wrote this down the other day (*produces a note pad from his desk*), and it's an amazing stat. If you count the season series against the four second division clubs in the American League -- namely the White Sox, Browns, Senators, and Athletics from 1930 to 1959 and then see how many season series each of these teams won against the Yankees in that span, the Browns won two, the Senators won two, and the White Sox and Athletics each won one. This means that over a thirty-year period, the composite season series record has the Yankees winning one hundred and fourteen and losing six. That's pathetic.

The economy of baseball, at least in the American League meant that these teams balanced their budgets, year after year, with two or three sellout home games against the Yankees. This is how the lesser teams would break even.

I think we are in better shape with more equal competition. I am sympathetic to the long suffering fans of the old franchises. I think Cub fans are the best there are, anywhere. They will turn out in enormous numbers even if the team is going nowhere, and their feel for the nature of baseball is exactly right. They are highly critical and they always know why the team isn't doing well. I've heard team owners and front office people say that they wish they had the Cub fans. But you want to see people like that rewarded. I remember when the Padres won in 1984, I was a little hard on the San Diego fans because they really hadn't been involved. They had never finished above fourth place, and regular season games were like exhibition games for them.

Q. Why do the Red Sox inspire such literary output?

A. Everyone is aware of the Calvinist nature, that sense of foreboding that attaches itself to the Red Sox. The Red Sox have become chic, when they made the Series several years ago the Boston *Globe* put together a literary supplement on the team. Fans are fans, but the intelligentsia probably aren't quite the same as the regular fans, the dyed-in-the-wool Sox fans.

Q. I have a feeling that this year we have finally begun to forget about the troubles in baseball. Is this true?

A. I think everyone is tired of this stuff, but the collusion issue isn't over yet, we're waiting for the next ruling. The economic penalties on this issue have yet to be determined.

The drug issue has been diminished because people realize that when you have six hundred plus young men traveling around with a lot of money and not much experience, then drugs will be part of the scene. Drugs are an American problem and sports will have its degree of people with a drug problem. I think there is less of the notion — and this will be a great step forward if it is true — that ballplayers have to be role models. That asks too much of athletes. If we can't think of better role models for our children than athletes, we're not doing very well by our kids.

There may a strike in our future because all sorts of unresolved issues are welling up. For example, there is no serious drug testing plan now in place. The old plan worked pretty well and the Commissioner did away with it.

Q. What would you say is the greatest potential threat to baseball?

A. I think it's expansion. If they want to go up two more teams in order to make the National League equal to the American than that would seem acceptable. A massive expansion would dilute the game terribly.

If that happens we could also walk into another tier of playoff games, and that would damage baseball very seriously. It would do away with the significance of the daily schedule, where every game matters. If you divide the teams into three leagues and look at the records of the four teams in a possible Playoff in this configuration, what you find is pathetic. The whole season will be played just to eliminate a few bad teams, the way it's done in hockey. Baseball would lose much of its appeal if the day-to-day were rendered next to meaningless.

Q. If you could go to three games this year which would they be?

A. I am delighted that I could not possibly answer that question. If you ask me on the first of July I might have a better idea.

I know I'll be interested to see how the Blue Jays bounce back. I think fans were rough on them, forgetting that they lost two front-line players in Fernandez and Whitt the final week of the season. The A's and the Mariners will be fun to watch. The Red Sox will be interesting with all their young talent and the Yankees have added everything but pitching. The Mets have seven starters, probably too many.

Q. For a while I know you wrote film reviews for The New Yorker. *Do you think there are any great baseball films?*

A. The challenge is to make a movie look like a ballgame and to put people out there who can throw and run a little bit. I remember seeing Gary Cooper playing Lou Gehrig, which was hilarious. None of the guys in that movie could throw.

They now have actors who make a reasonable try at the game. You have the same problems with baseball films as with baseball fiction. I was disappointed that they changed the end of *The Natural*. This is an interesting novel, intertwining baseball and the King Arthur legend. The film had some beautifully shot scenes, but it made no sense, so they had to lay on the slow motion and fireworks at the end. I think that if you make a good movie with baseball in it, you're fine, but if you go out to make a baseball movie, you're in trouble.

Q. Have you ever cheered in the press box?

A. Oh, sure. I've been in press boxes where there has been a lot of cheering. The regular writers pretend that they're above this sort of thing, but they don't fool anyone.

Q. Has SABRmetrics been overdone?

A. I don't think it's an issue. Overdone for whom? Some people love this stuff. It's an addition to the game, it's a different way of looking at it. I don't think it changes how the game is played. I don't think the front offices use SABRmetrics. I think Bill James' stuff and SABRmetrics is a lot of fun, but it doesn't mean much to me because I'm not mathematically minded. I'm amused by this stuff and I read Bill James with awe, but it doesn't change how I think about the game.

Q. Do you find it sad to see so many of our baseball heroes going to shopping malls and selling their autographs?

A. I find it very sad. I think that this is one of the great arguments for increased pension benefits for older players. There is a good organization which includes Ralph Branca that assists former players in need.

In many ways I'm not happy at Old Timers' Games. The players enjoy it, they have a big laugh, but I don't like to see someone whom I remember as a great outfielder hobbling along to beat out a nubbed roller. We know they're old now, but seeing them as they are now interferes with our memory of what they were in their youth. It's warming to see them, but it's embarrassing.

We want to make an exhibition out of everything, we want everything to be immediately accessible, but some things are better left to memory and imagination.

The instant replay is great for understanding but it diminishes the moment. You see a great play and you jump up and say, "WOW!" and you can't get over it. But you see it on replay and you say, "Oh, that's how it happened" and you see it a third time and it's become only interesting. The wonder of it, the brilliance has gone out of it.

Q. Were you disappointed when you moved from your perch in the grandstand to the field and met your heroes?

A. Sure, absolutely, but I don't wish it otherwise. I'm a reporter. Some people say that I'm a poet or an essay writer, but I view myself as a reporter. Reporters learn the truth about people. I'm a grown-up, and I don't care if a great ballplayer is not a great guy. We go to a game to see what these guys do, or don't do out on the field. What they're like in the clubhouse, how they treat their wives or how they think about Nicaragua are totally beside the point and usually not very interesting. We sometimes forget what we came for. People become so famous that we want to be close to them and know everything about them. We want their fame rather than what they can do. Reggie played the press like a Stradivarius and understood all this. He was a natural showman. He also drove me crazy, like everyone else, but I believe that Reggie operated under more self-imposed pressure than any player I've ever seen. Those three home runs in the '77 Series was the greatest baseball feat I've witnessed. His persona has eclipsed what he was as a player and that is a loss. It's too bad.

Q. What constructive things can SABR do for baseball?

A. I think that the way for SABR to be most effective would be to try to enroll all the significant front office people and deluge them with material. They should be more aware of the existence of the people of SABR and their care for the game. I think the ballparks committee is great, but I would be surprised if any owner really paid close attention to the committee when he was getting ready to build a new ballpark. And they should. There is no reason why baseball can't build a modern Wrigley Field or Fenway Park, a jewel with all the charm of the parks built in 1912, and the modern amenities as well.

But I don't think most owners think like this or think about these possibilities. If the Giants had won the right to build that new downtown ballpark I'm not sure if Bob Lurie would have listened to people with strong feelings about baseball. Owners think they own the game when all they own is a franchise. The fans are really the owners of the game.

He would begin to tell a story and talk the player's foot right off the bag and then tag him.

The Voices
of Fans
By David L. Ulin

THE NEIGHBORHOOD OF BASEBALL, by Barry Gifford
San Francisco: Donald S. Ellis/Creative Arts Books Co., 1985
$7.95 (paper)

FATHERS PLAYING CATCH WITH SONS, by Donald Hall
New York: Dell/Laurel Books, 1986. $3.95 (paper)

THIS PAST FEBRUARY, THE CITY OF CHICAGO FINALLY yielded to massive pressure from the Commissioner's office and the Tribune company and decided to put lights in Wrigley Field. The City Council tried to mask the significance of the move by claiming that there would be a minimum number of games played at night, thereby completely missing the point of the issue. And although I would be the first to admit that Wrigley Field with lights is better than no Wrigley Field at all, I can't help but feel something akin to a burning pain in my gut every time I contemplate the defacement of Wrigley, for such a defacement illustrates once again a certain lack of respect on the part of the men who run Major League baseball for the voices of fans.

Actually, the most immediate result of the announcement to light Wrigley was that I went running for my copy of Barry Gifford's *The Neighborhood of Baseball*, a wonderfully personal account of what it was like to grow up as a Cub fan in the 1950's and early 1960's. As I read through it again my appreciation grew, for now that Wrigley is to be forced so indelicately into the 1980's, Gifford's book has become more than a memoir, but a little piece of history as well. And it is a book that is well suited to such a challenge. For those of us who have seen Wrigley in her unlit glory, *The Neighborhood of Baseball* will bring back memories; for those who missed it, this book may become all that's left of that great and longstanding Chicago tradition of weekday baseball. In either case, as a personal account of a boy's love affair with a baseball team, it is unmatched in the annals of baseball literature.

Gifford opens *The Neighborhood of Baseball* with a measurement: "I was born in 1946, one year after the Chicago Cubs last won the National League pennant." It is significant that in the period the book covers (it was first published in 1981), the Cubs did nothing substantial to bring another pennant home to Chicago. Particularly during the seasons from 1952 to 1964 that Gifford attended "aproximately fifty. . .games a year," the Cubs set a standard of futility and mediocrity challenged only by such teams as the old St. Louis Browns. But it is also significant that the measurement Gifford presents is one of his own life against the history of the team to which he is allied. In that statement, we understand right off the voice with which this story will be told, a voice that will find itself in its connection to some larger other, the voice of the fan. Gifford himself refers to this early in the book, when he describes his first experience at Wrigley Field: "The Cubs won, I remember that, they looked good...It was a proper beginning for a young fan...I see it now as being a bit like the lure and dilemma of the South Seas for Gauguin, all that overwhelming beauty with nary an early sign of the insidious secret to be one day suddenly revealed in all its irrevocable and horrible truth." For Gifford, that secret is the overwhelming mediocrity of the team that would come to occupy his child's life.

But a case can be made that it is precisely this mediocrity, and the ensuing frustration of the fan, that forges so strong a bond between boy and team. Certainly the rite of fanhood is an important part of many American childhoods, and most of us grow up rooting for less than worldbeaters. Yet somewhere in there with the mediocrity and the frustration must be a strong dose of acceptance, or no one would continue to follow their team year after year. The failures of our heroes on the field prepare us for the constant battle of later life, the temporary victories and partial setbacks, the ebb and flow of events that progress much like the long but finite run of games in a season. Baseball, it has been said, is a lot like life precisely because there is so much failure built into both. And although some teams seem to wear futility like a crown, every fan should relate on some personal level to the tribulations Gifford describes, for all of our bonds have survived great frustrations.

The Cubs, however, are something else again, a team whose consistent lack of success has involved fans of all ages in "as unrequited a relationship [as] anyone could have with a ball club." To convey both the child's hopeful resignation and the adult's sense of tragic loyalty, Gifford divides *The Neighborhood of Baseball* into two formally and contextually distinct sections that work alone but only achieve full meaning together. Part I, "The Past Recaptured," ties together the strands of his season-by-season devotion to the Cubs. In a sense, this is Gifford's autobiography in baseball. He begins with the team, then shifts focus to his life as a child, introducing his grandfather, Ezra, "who had a candy stand under the Addison Street elevated tracks near Wrigley Field," and his parents, and the city of Chicago, so that we already identify with him by the time baseball returns to define the story. Gifford's command of timing and detail fosters these connections, and once he has us, he brings us into his relationship with his team.

Indeed, the beauty of "The Past Recaptured" is in its loving recollections of a boy's baseball obsessions. Gifford is quick to develop the kind of gallows humor a Cub fan needs, and although he writes with the benefit of many years of hindsight, there is the strong sense that, in this situation, hindsight and foresight are not so far removed. Witness what he has to say about seeing then-Cub Lou Brock record his first major league hit in September 1961: "[In] his first at bat...he bounced a single up the middle. I...could hardly have guessed that before [he] was through he'd have added better than 3000 more...What I might have predicted, however, was that he'd get most of them for a team other than the Cubs." But as potent as this material may be, it requires an additional connective fiber to give it meaning in the context of Gifford's present life. And it is Part II, "The Past Sustained," that provides this fiber and uncovers the true story of *The Neighborhood of Baseball*. In so doing, it gives the book a greater depth. For "The Past Sustained" is about what Gifford calls "a kind of religious reprise." It describes a trip he took to Chicago in August 1980 to sit in the bleachers for a week or two and reconnect with the ghosts of his past, "those...fabled men and boys I'd never met yet knew so intimately...[men of] yesterday, a day that for me and Big Steve and countless others had never ended." In attempting this, Gifford validates the past in a way that less self-conscious methods cannot achieve. After all, if the past is physically gone, it continues to exist inside each of us, altered to fit our own specifications but alive nonetheless. Yet without connection to the present, it can only atrophy. For those who respect the past, therefore, it is a constant battle to maintain its relevance.

And that is the battle that Gifford engages in here. Much of "The Past Sustained" is caught up in the details of those 1980 Cubs and of Gifford's brief but intense firsthand exposure to them. But Gifford takes those details and turns them into something else. A particularly testy response by the Wrigley regulars to Dave Kingman T-shirt day becomes a chance for Gifford to ruminate on the reasons for such animosity, reasons that date back to his own childhood.

The 1985 edition of *The Neighborhood of Baseball* features a preface written over the course of the 1984 season, and in just a couple of pages, we see the author go from elation to complete dejection. It is even worse, Gifford seems to be saying, to come away with nothing after being as close as the Cubs were in 1984. But even in this darkest of moments, the dream of fanhood goes on. Gifford mentions that his daughter Phoebe watched Game Five of the 1984 Playoffs with him and that she was confident until the end that the Cubs would pull it out. Unstated is the premise that the team's failure to do so represents another rite of passage for both father and child in the neighborhood of baseball. For Gifford, the Cubs' ignominious defeat lifts his own ingrained patterns of frustration and resignation to a higher level. For his daughter, it is an introduction to the true nature of fanhood in general and Cub fanhood in particular. But for both of them, in a way, it is an affirmation, for the worst has happened, and although tested, their loyalties remain strong and in place.

And yet loyalties continue to be tested. The Cubs are a last place team again in 1988, a position to which their fans have grown accustomed over the years. Now, however, the old ballpark, Wrigley Field, is to be modernized in an act of sacrilege that Gifford could not have anticipated seven years ago. To me, that ballpark has always been the neighborhood of baseball, for "neighborhood" carries with it associations of children playing ball in the street on a long summer day, associations of innocence and timelessness that are the greater part of Wrigley Field. At midsummer home games, the stands fill up with school children on vacation and businessmen reaching back into their youth to play hookey once again. This will not happen at night. The game at night is less magical; it is for adults. And although it remains to be seen to what extent night baseball will take over on the North Side of Chicago, its presence at all will make the game more of an entertainment and less a part of life.

In any case, there will always be Gifford's book. Taken as either memoir or history, it is an excellent entry into the life and mind of a fan, a man who defines his life in some very real sense by measuring it against the team that he loves. In Gifford's view, the act of fanhood begins in a relationship with a specific team; his book is a celebration of this belief and of all the attendant emotions and attachments that accompany it. In the neighborhood of baseball, he is telling us, it is enough simply to belong.

But what of another type of fan, he or she who is more involved with the sport as a whole than with any particular team? These fans, by and large, are older, and have moved through the years from specificity to generality in their rooting. For them, it seems less important to belong than to appreciate. Even so, their connection to the game takes its form in an attachment to a number of teams rather than to the whole of baseball itself. It is as if the totality of the sport is too much for any one heart to encompass, leaving even those who love the game for itself to find anchor in some degree of specific expression.

One such fan is the poet Donald Hall, and his particular brand of appreciation is collected in *Fathers Playing Catch with Sons*, a diverse and thoughtful volume of essays that focus mainly on baseball. Hall's own tenuous loyalties belong to the Red Sox, the Pirates, the Tigers, and the Brooklyn Dodgers, whose move west set him on the path to baseball pantheism. Now, as he says in his introduction, "I do not need particular teams: the game's the thing." The body of his book goes on to celebrate the many different levels and areas of the game, and, indeed, to celebrate the act of celebrating itself.

Hall's best essay is the title piece, "Fathers Playing Catch with Sons," which opens the book and recounts a week Hall spent in March 1973 as a participant in spring training with the Pittsburgh Pirates. The writing here plays well, illustrating as it does the peculiar irony of an overweight middle-aged poet cavorting like a kid and staring awestruck as the likes of Willie Stargell and Dock Ellis prepare for the long season ahead. In fact, it is Hall's own appreciation of the absurdity of his position that gives this essay its substance. After all, many baseball fans harbor similar fantasies to those Hall acts out here; most of us, however, are too sensible or too inhibited to act upon them. And yet here is a man attempting to break down that final barrier between fan and athlete and, at the same time, letting us in to witness the process. We readers and fellow fans cannot help but laugh, at the same time shaking our heads in admiration for the sheer unbridled courage of this man. For it is a courage that comes from love of the game, from the fan's universal desire to see deeper into the layers and textures of baseball and come away with a broader understanding. As such, it is a courage that we may not share but can certainly understand.

There is melancholy in "Fathers Playing Catch with Sons," but it is not the expected melancholy of an older man trying to achieve what never could have been; it is instead represented by Hall's encounters with Luke Wrenn, an eighteen year-old player with no chance of making the team. As we read Hall's conversations with Luke, it slowly dawns on us that this, too, is what professional baseball is about: the dreams of a young athlete whose athletic prime will not be enough and the appreciation of a middle-aged man in uniform at last. Yet there is nothing wrong with such melancholy; it is a part of the way things have always been, for the player and for the fan. After all, Hall reminds us, "baseball is continuous...an endless game of repeated summers, joining the long generations of all the fathers and all the sons." And there is plenty of room in such a continuity: room for melancholy and for celebration and for all the things that come in between.

There is also room for further adventures, and Hall describes these in a second essay, "The Country Of Baseball," which recounts his return to the Pirates in 1974, this time as an observer. It is here that Hall's true obsessions and appreciations come to the fore and that his own conception of fanhood takes shape and finds expression. And the cornerstone of this conception is his belief in baseball as the substance of myth. "Baseball is a country all to itself," Hall writes. "It is an old country...Steam locomotives puff across trestles and through tunnels. It is...miniature with distance and old age. The citizens wear baggy pinstripes, knickers, and caps. Seasons and teams shift, blur into each other...Citizens retire to farms...and all at once they are young players again, lean and intense, running the base paths with filed spikes."

Myth, however, is only effective in its relation to reality, a fact Hall understands and integrates into his essay. There is the story of the night that Dock Ellis set a major league record by hitting the first (and only) three batters he faced. As Hall records it: "They were the first three batters up, in the first inning. They were Cincinnati Reds batters. Dock's control was just fine." To Hall, such an act fits in perfectly with the myth-making apparatus of the game, for it is an act that is larger than life, that goes beyond the participants and the observers to become a part of baseball's lore. Hall makes sure to phrase it in the proper terms: "In the country of baseball, pitchers are always throwing baseballs at batters."

The other pieces in *Fathers Playing Catch with Sons* are mostly short pieces, ephemera: an ode to Fenway Park here, a brief and shining image of the Cracker Jack Old Timers Baseball Classic there, and two striking essays about baseball writing that in their humor and appreciation reveal as much about the literature of the sport as anything I have ever seen. But perhaps Hall's own views are spoken most clearly in the closing paragraph to another essay, "Baseball And The Meaning Of Life." "Baseball," he writes, "sets off the meaning of life precisely because it is pure of meaning. As the ripples in the sand (in the Kyoto garden) organize and formalize the dust which is dust, so the diamond and rituals of baseball create an elegant, trivial, enchanted grid on which our suffering, shapeless, sinful day leans for the momentary grid of order." The same is true of myth, or of anything that we use as an organizing principle in our lives. For Donald Hall, it is baseball that fills this role, baseball in its purest state. His is the mythical game, played in the interior stadium, in the country of baseball that is a part of every fan.

So what does all this mean? Well, to me it means that baseball is still a fan's game, no matter what happens to it. And fanhood is as illusory a thing as a good knuckleball or a .300 batting average. Perhaps it is this that is most wonderful about baseball, the fact that so many people can watch the game for so long and still come up with so many ways of appreciating it. Yet for all this we must still be careful. Baseball is a neighborhood, or it is a country. It is most certainly a thing of great value, a fact that both *The Neighborhood of Baseball* and *Fathers Playing Catch with Sons* celebrate. The value, however, resides in its little details as much as in its larger movements, and as we move further along, it is precisely these details that seem to become expendable. The lighting of Wrigley Field is just the latest example. Perhaps Donald Hall is right when he says that "the country remains the same," but some things, once lost, are not retrievable. It is up to us, the fans, to keep the actual game, the neighborhood game, as like as possible to the mythical game. For in the country of baseball, the game may be all we have, but, by the same token, we are all the game has. It is all connected.

And it is out of this connection that these two books speak to us. In their pages, we hear our own stories, our own myths, our own voices. We hear the voices of fans.

Copyright ©1988, by David L. Ulm

Mostly McGraw

by Louis D. Rubin, Jr.

JOHN McGRAW
By Charles C. Alexander
New York: The Viking Press, 1988. $19.95 clothbound

IN ONE OF ERNEST HEMING-way's Nick Adams stories, "The Three-Day Blow," two youths are sitting out a storm in a cabin in Michigan, and a section of the dialogue goes like this:

"What did the Cards do?"

"Dropped a double-header to the Giants."

"That ought to cinch it for them."

"It's a gift," Bill said. "As long as McGraw can buy every good ballplayer in the league there's nothing to it."

"He can't buy them all," Nick said.

"He can buy the ones he wants," Bill said. "Or he makes them discontented so they have to trade them to him."

"Like Heinie Zim," Nick agreed.

"That bonehead will do him a lot of good."

Bill stood up.

"He can hit," Nick offered. The heat from the fire was baking his legs.

"He's a sweet fielder, too," Bill said. "But he loses ball games."

"Maybe that's what McGraw wants him for," Nick suggested.

"Maybe," Bill agreed.

"There's always more to it than we know about," Nick said.

Hemingway was not really a close student of major league baseball -- in *The Sun Also Rises* he spells Frank Frisch's last name 'Fritch' -- but it isn't difficult to spot the reference to the purchase of Heinie Zimmerman by the New York Giants in 1916, after the Chicago third-baseman had so irked Manager Joe Tinker by his lackadaisical behavior that he had been given a ten-day suspension. The pennant race could only have been that of the year following, 1917, when McGraw's Giants won and the Cardinals finished third. Zimmerman did help his new club that year, hitting .297 and driving in 102 runs, but two years later he was dropped by McGraw and then permanently banned from the game for having tried to bribe Larry Benton and Bennie Kauff to throw ballgames.

What is interesting about the passage in Hemingway's story is the glimpse it offers of John McGraw's contemporary reputation. Presumably the two youths are Chicago Cub fans -- Hemingway grew up in suburban Oak Park. Resentment of McGraw for purchasing the baseball talent he needed to win pennants was widespread, especially among followers of the Cubs, who were the Giants' principal National League rivals throughout the late 1900s and the 1910s.

More than once McGraw was accused of tampering with opposing players, hinting to them that he wanted to acquire their services, with the result that the players in question allegedly began sulking and ceased to play their best, in hopes of thereby making their teams willing to sell or trade them to the Giants. For the New York Giants were the most consistently successful and prosperous club of the Dead Ball Era, and McGraw's players not only could count on frequent shares in World Series gate receipts but were the best salaried performers of their time.

All this and much more is described in Charles Alexander's new biography of John McGraw, who as Alexander says was major league baseball's most notable figure prior to Babe Ruth's emergence into full glory and the rise of the Yankees in the early 1920s. Connie Mack, whose Philadelphia teams twice bested McGraw's Giants in World Series play during the period, declared in 1927 that "There has been only one McGraw, and there has been only one manager -- and his name [is] McGraw." Between 1903, his first full season as skipper of the Giants, and 1924, when he won his last pennant, his team led the National League ten times, finished second eight times, and only once ended a season out of the first division.

Throughout that period he was caught up in controversy. There was nothing (or in any event very little) about him that was lovable. If it was Leo Durocher who actually voiced that unforgettable sentiment, "Nice guys finish last," John McGraw was the incarnation of the attitude thus expressed. He terrorized umpires in ways that even an Earl Weaver later forebore to do, he tyrannized over his players, he employed foul language and distasteful epithet beyond even the best efforts of Dr. Durocher, he was a rotten loser, he regularly associated with gamblers and touts, he played dirty baseball and encouraged his players to do so. Though never convicted of offering bribes to opposing players, he tolerated shady characters like Zimmerman and Hal Chase on his teams and there were enough actual allegations of scandal close to him to make one wonder at times whether there were any limits to what the man would not do in order to win a pennant. On the ball field he was decidedly nobody's Nice Guy -- and he won ball games and pennants more consistently than any of his contemporaries.

Yet he was generous, and to a fault; how much money he disbursed in handouts to needy ex-ballplayers will never be known. He was loyal; he stuck by his friends. Off the field he was affable, charming, even easygoing (except sometimes when drunk.) Frank Frisch, who starred for him, broke with him after absorbing more and worse verbal abuse than he could endure, and later became his friend once again, described the difference as being "night and day off the field from what he was on the field."

Like his previous book on Ty Cobb, Alexander's biography is solidly researched, capably written, and informative throughout. He follows McGraw from his somewhat disadvantaged beginnings, his entry into professional baseball, and his steady acquisition of the skills needed for successful major league competition. The years on Ned Hanlon's Baltimore Orioles were filled with controversy and tumult. The scrappy little Irishman's very-few-holds-barred style epitomized the combative ways of that famous club at the close of an era when the modern game was just coming into being and the structure of organized ball was still tentative and uncertain. Described at length are the often-tortuous and not always above-board dealings whereby, first in league with and then in fierce opposition to Ban Johnson, McGraw ended up in 1902 as manager of Andy Freedman's New York National League club.

Thereafter the fortunes of the "Little Napoleon" and his ball team are chronicled by the season. Alexander makes a fundamental point about McGraw's way of operation. He did not think in terms of the future; he did not take the long view. Each of his ball clubs was put together with a single eye toward winning that year's pennant. If midway through a season the Giants needed help at a particular position or positions, he bought or traded for the required skills. The Giants drew well, he had the money to afford the best, and he did not hesitate to spend it.

If ever a manager's imprint was upon a team, John McGraw's was on the old New York Giants. Christy Mathewson declared that "the club is McGraw." Even his enemies, and they were numerous, readily testified to his managerial genius. If one considers

McGraw's pennant-winning personnel, whether the three-times-victorious 1911-1913 club or the four-time 1921-1924 champions, it is obvious that he never fielded "great" ball teams, in the manner of the 1911-1914 Philadelphia A's, the Red Sox of the 1910s, or the Yankee clubs of the middle and late 1920s. Mathewson was his only real "superstar." His lineups changed from year to year. The personnel available for each successive season presented a new set of problems to be solved; and more often than not McGraw found the solutions.

What I miss in this excellent biography of a colorful and important figure are two things. More attention might have been given to how McGraw managed -- how he handled his pitchers, how he sought to score runs, how he plotted his defenses. Surely there must exist contemporary accounts of particular ball games that would illustrate McGraw in action as manager. There is a great deal here about McGraw's competitiveness, and about his skill in coming up with key personnel, but not enough about his day-to-day handling of his players and his tactics.

And I could wish that Alexander had given us more anecdotes. So much of the charm of baseball history lies in the personalities of the players themselves. As excellent as this work is, its lack of humor and anecdotage means it is less than it could be. The columns of The Sporting News, Baseball Magazine, and the newspapers of the period must surely be loaded with incidents and remarks and exploits that, judiciously gleaned, could have enriched this book. I get the sense that Alexander takes baseball history a trifle too seriously; he seems not to enjoy the inherent comedy as well as he might.

Yet do not misunderstand; this biography is a fine job of literary craftsmanship. It contains no hyperbole, and is without crap. It details, sensibly and tastefully, a baseball career and an era. It does not merely recount, but interprets. Insofar as useful baseball books go, it is worth several dozen "as told to's," impressionistic evocations of the supposed Age of Titans, or compilations of statistical data. If the price of this kind of sober, competent detailing of the subject is insufficient comedy and taletelling, then it is a shortcoming, as they say, up with which we will all gladly put.

The Early Game -- By the Masters

By Ed Goldstein

AMERICA'S NATIONAL GAME by A.G. Spalding
New York: American Sports Publishing, 1911. 542 pp.

MANY READERS OF THIS edition of *The SABR Review of Books* are familiar with the review of *Pitching in a Pinch* that appeared in the second number of this series. Part of it detailed the reviewer's dogged and ultimately successful search for an authentic hard-cover copy of the book from the early years of this century. I was interested in that book as well, and searched, with somewhat less vigor for a hardcover copy in vain. As so often happens, my search ended when I wandered into my favorite used bookstore without any particular goal in mind. Apparently, some longtime baseball fan had liquidated his personal library, and several volumes had reached the dealer. I recognized "Pitching" immediately. Another volume was less familiar. A thick, squat book with faded gold lettering on the spine rested inches from Matty's work. When I pulled it from the shelf, there stood Uncle Sam himself on the front cover, bat in hand, under the words "America's National Game." On the bottom of the cover, the author's name, A.G. Spalding. Words to conjure by, if any exist in baseball literature. For those who are interested, I purchased both for the grand total of $6.50, proving that there are still bargains to be had for those who are patient enough.

The story behind *America's National Game* is as interesting as the book itself. Spalding was, in 1911, what Connie Mack was to become to later generations, "The Grand Old Man of Baseball." Starting in the years immediately following the Civil War, Spalding had been an outstanding amateur pitcher for the famous Forest City club of Rockford, Illinois, one of the first professionals in the early 1870s, organizer and participant in baseball's world tours of the 1870s and 1880s, co-founder of the National League in 1876, founder of the most famous sporting goods manufacturer of its time and a leading spokesman and authority for the game, even after nearly being elected to the U.S. Senate. All of the above notwithstanding, Spalding had declined to put his recollections of the game's history on paper, deferring to his mentor "Father" Henry Chadwick, the first great baseball writer, and inventor of the boxscore and baseball statistics. Chadwick's later years were marked by declining health, and just before his death in 1908 he realized that he would never be able to produce the single great work he and Spalding had discussed. At Chadwick's death, the old man's entire baseball archives were delivered to Spalding by Chadwick's widow, who told Spalding of Chadwick's desire that he complete the work. *America's National Game* is based to some extent on Chadwick's archives, but it is not the book that Chadwick would have written. To his credit, Spalding admits as much.

For all his mid-nineteenth century country bumpkin upbringing, Spalding the man was a shrewd and successful businessman, who had parlayed his fame as a ballplayer and entrepreneur into a sizable personal fortune and political career. He had several axes to grind, and he hones them pretty well in this book of almost 550 pages.

To understand the importance of this book as an historical record, the reader must keep the publishing date firmly in mind. Three recent successful baseball books, *The Ultimate Baseball Book*, and Honig's companion *The American League* and *The National League*, both begin with the year 1900. Spalding's book gives accounts, and in most cases eyewitness accounts of the author or his associates, of the game as it existed to the mid-1840's. The bulk of the book is finished before the founding of the American League in 1900 is even mentioned. All the World Series up to that time are dismissed in two pages.

The only part of the book that could truly be characterized as Chadwick's is that part dealing with amateur organized Base Ball (the sport is always referred to with two capitalized words throughout the book) in the years from 1840 to 1865. For this portion, the book is a gold mine of information for anyone interested in the true infancy of the national sport.

The rest of the book is Spalding's. This is not necessarily to imply that it is an inferior portion, but that the focus changes from narrative of the game's evolution to an explanation of his own motives and an apologia for the conduct of the game's business from one of the game's foremost businessmen. To begin with, we are given the original and definitive story of Abner Doubleday and the Cooperstown myth, as told by its foremost proponent. Spalding was horrified to hear anyone imply that the manly American game of baseball could have evolved from that most British of sports, cricket; or worse from the British schoolgirls' pastime, rounders. Spalding therefore headed a commission of like-minded "researchers" who solicited the recollections of any old men in the period just after the turn of the century who could possibly remember when they first observed the game. Somehow they arrived at Doubleday, Cooperstown, and 1839. Spalding even mentions Oliver Wendell Holmes' recollection of playing baseball at Harvard in 1829, but glosses over it without explanation.

For the period 1865 to about 1885 we learn scraps and scratches of information about what was happening in the game. If a player was not a teammate or employee of Spalding (Cap Anson or Mike Kelly, for example) we hear nothing of him. Spalding is much more concerned with letting his reader know about his own travels through the world of baseball, the troubles and sorrows of owning a baseball club, how Spalding and William Hulbert conceived and founded the National League, and how the founding of that League forever eradicated gambling and alcoholism from the game (this from a book written eight years before the Black Sox scandal.) This is not to be dismissed as irrelevant or incorrect. But the reader must keep in mind that the author has a reputation to uphold, and an entire game to protect.

The remainder of the book is Spalding's recounting of how the game has spread through the colleges, the military and around the world to America's colonies (such as Cuba and the Philippines) and to its trading partners (Japan is reported to be developing a pretty good game.) All of this is reported in a condescending tone, especially towards the Oriental and Hispanic peoples in their attempt to adopt America's Game.

Which leads us to criticism of the book, one minor, one possibly major, and more a criticism of the times it was written than the book itself. The prose style of the book borders on the ponderous. 1911 was still the era of grand oratory, when public speakers were expected to harangue a crowd for hours on end whether they had anything to say or not. Spalding, as a public figure and the game's truly official spokesman sometimes goes on a length when brevity would do. But this is the tone of the time, and if anything A.G. was being restrained.

A more serious note comes when Spalding talks about the founding of the Cincinnati Red Stockings and public reaction to them. He refers to the objections of the fans of the amateur game to paid ballplayers as stemming from their desire to see "gentlemen" play the game; that if paid competition became the order of the day, a player would be hired "without regard to his race, color, or previous condition of servitude." Spalding's ironic reference to the Fourteenth Amendment to the Constitution reminds us that it was in his era, and at the instigation of his friend and colleague Anson, that America's National Game became White America's Game. The fair horizon that Spalding paints in his book is shadowed for the modern reader by the dark cloud of racial separation that hovered over the game until 35 years after his death. Spalding, as the major figure representing the organized game at this time must be held responsible with many others for allowing this to come about.

But this is the one dark cloud in what is otherwise a sunny revelation for anyone not familiar with baseball's earliest days. Anyone seeking to learn about William Hulbert, the driving force behind the modern baseball league (and curiously absent from the Hall of Fame); the insider's view of the Player's League struggle of 1889-91; the life of the nineteenth century ballplayer, ballclub owner or league official; or many other views of a baseball time long gone, will profit from a reading of *America's National Game*. Photographs of incredible historical interest, the cartoons of Homer Davenport (many of which have been produced in the pages of *The SABR Review of Books*) and, last but not least, a complete account of the Arctic Whaling Fleet's mid-winter baseball league, played on the frozen surface of Herschel Island Cove at −47°F, make this a book worth seeking out and reading.

The Subject and the Voice

By Bill James

ROWDY RICHARD by Dick Bartell and Norman Macht
Berkeley, CA: North Atlantic Books, 1987. $18.95

THERE IS A GREAT DEAL to be said for the concept which underlies *Rowdy Richard*. Rowdy Richard Bartell was a shortstop who played 18 years in the major leagues; 18 years, if you count two at bats in 1927 and two in 1946 as a year apiece. At the time he was called Rowdy Dick more often than Rowdy Richard, but the nickname, having become salacious through no fault of its occupant, has been modified into the more polite form which is the title of the recent biography with collaborator Norman Macht. Bartell was a pretty good hitter, hit .300 six times, a good baserunner and a salty shortstop who was as good defensively as almost anybody he played against. There are worse players in the Hall of Fame.

Now, when there is a meeting in the New York City offices of a publishing giant, and they are wondering what they can do to make some money, nobody is going to say "why don't we do a biography of one of the second-line baseball stars of the 1930s, like maybe Dick Bartell or Billy Rogell? I'll bet he's got some interesting stories to tell, and he's probably got more time to sit down with a collaborator than Don Mattingly does." Their instinct is to look at the spotlight, at the player who is hot at this moment in this big city. The economic trick is to catch a ride on the free publicity.

The economic formula, of course, is not calculated to produce a good book, for the hot star of the Mets of the moment is most likely a 23-year-old kid with two years of junior college and so much pressure on him that he has about eight to ten hours to spend with his collaborator, sharing all the wisdom and perspective of his experience. There is a great deal to be said for the idea of looking away from the publicity, looking to the past, looking to the man who was just as good a player at a forgotten time in a little-remembered place, but who has had the time to ripen his understanding of what it all meant, and who now has the time to share that understanding with us.

And Bartell does, indeed, have some good stories. Baseball legend has it that the long train rides of the pre-1950 era were a source of camaraderie among old-time players, who had all those hours together in which to talk baseball. Bartell tells about a handful of teammates with the Pirates of the late twenties who got drunk and went through the train tearing up bathrooms and breaking out windows like primeval rock stars, and then put the arm on their teammates to help pay for the damage. Bartell antied up once, but they just did it again, and when he refused to contribute again they were pretty unhappy with him. He names names, in this incident and others, but I reckon you ought to have to buy the book to get some of those.

Pie Traynor, of all people, is reported as stealing a milkman's horsedrawn wagon and racing it down Broadway at 2 a.m. with the police in pursuit. Bartell recounts encounters with the aging Barney Dreyfuss, a man who never met a dollar bill he didn't want to keep, and the declining John McGraw, whose attempts to control the team were growing more frantic as his grasp of the game was slipping. Bartell truly loathes Dreyfuss, unforgiven after all these years.

In fact, Bartell in his later years remains a little rowdy. The list of people that he doesn't like is substantial; it includes Pie Traynor ("Traynor was a nice guy, but nasty nice...he protected Pie Traynor first"), Burleigh Grimes ("The players hated him"), Rogers Hornsby ("Hornsby had no feelings and didn't believe anybody else did, either"), most of his managers and an assortment of teammates, umpires, reporters and front office executives. Not that this is necessarily a negative; indeed, a healthy mean streak is one of the main things a publisher looks for in a potential biography subject.

I have never read a biography so much of which takes place outside the viewing of the supposed subject. There are stories in the book from the nineteenth century and from the 1960s, all supposedly tied in some oblique way to the career of Dick Bartell. When he hits upon a story you haven't heard before this is kind of fun, but for the most part these stories have been retreaded so often that there is just nothing left in them. Once more McCarthy smashes the card table in the Yankee clubhouse with his axe (Bartell was in the other league), once more Fred Lindstrom is crushed by his failure to get the manager's job when McGraw retires, once more John T. Brush's barber recommends Fred Merkle for the Giants. One groans when once more the bird flies from underneath the hat of Casey Stengel (Bartell was eleven years old at the time.) Hundreds of people are mentioned in the book that Bartell probably never met, people like Moses Solomon, Hughie Jennings, Jake Beckley, Charlie Comiskey, Cap Anson and Fred Toney. Sometimes they are dragged in for an anecdote, sometimes for a quick profile. Even when dealing with Bartell's contemporaries, the stories often involve games of the Cubs against the Phillies when Bartell was playing for the Giants. Want to read about the Babe Herman three-men-on-third incident again? I'm not talking about getting a little off the track here, but about losing the track. I know that at least 40% of this book takes place in times and places when Bartell simply couldn't have been there, and it might be 70%.

The account of Cleveland crybabies incident is interesting in that Bartell seems to have a personal slant on it, and the recounting of the suicide of Willard Hershberger is somewhat interesting, in that Macht seems to have researched it well. The problem is not that he researches anything poorly, but that he researches everything indiscriminately, producing no depth in understanding anything.

One of the most critical steps in planning a successful book is deciding what the reader knows and what he doesn't know. If you waste the reader's time telling him things that he already knows, he is going to be irritated. If you assume he knows things that he doesn't, he's going to be lost. Macht, in my opinion, completely failed to think through the issue. It should be obvious, I would think, that anybody who is going to be reading the biography of a baseball player whose best years were more than a half-century ago is already knowledgeable about baseball and baseball history. A casual baseball fan is going to start with the Honig books or contemporary biographies or the annual edition of *Who's Who in Baseball*; he is not going to start with the biography of the fourth-best shortstop of the 1930s. Macht winds up writing to people who aren't reading. Two pages are given over to another recounting of the circumstances surrounding Babe Ruth's called shot in the 1932 World Series, although Bartell never stops to say "Oh, by the way, I was there," presumably because he wasn't. It is incomprehensible that there could be anybody reading this book who doesn't already know that story.

I have also never read a biography in which the voice of the putative subject and the voice of the collaborator remained so distinct. At first this is very confusing, as you try to figure out how Bartell knows all of this stuff. Has he become a baseball historian in the thirty years since he left the game? After about twenty pages, however, you become (or I became, at least) acutely aware of when Bartell is speaking about his experiences, and when Macht is retelling something he has read. At times the subject and the collaborator seem to be almost at war. While Bartell delivers a diatribe against statistics, Macht quotes obscure statistics as if he were being paid by the digit (Burgess Whitehead in 1936 handled the third highest number of chances ever by a second baseman, 1,026, while Tony Cuccinello lost the batting title in 1945 by .30854 to .30845. It was actually .30846, but what the hey; we don't want to get carried away with these meaningless statistics.) Bartell, as an old player, wants to break out and tell why baseball in his era was so much better than it is now--but Macht, as a historian, knows that old ballplayers have been saying that since 1860, and no intelligent person is going to take it seriously. As you read the resulting section, you can hear them debating the issue.

Bartell lets us know what he thinks about the relative quality of today's play, game-winning RBI, sabermetrics, the amount of attention given to home-run hitters rather than good defensive players and the quality of official scorers. His opinions on all of these subjects are precisely what you would have assumed they were anyway if he hadn't said anything about it, and one suspects that the only reason he lets fly with these opinions is to preserve his amateur standing as an intellectual, despite having written a book and all. *Rowdy Richard* is the biography of a man who has lived a long and interesting life, and has learned damned near nothing from it. His All-Star team of the players he saw includes only one post-war player, Roberto Clemente. At shortstop he would have Travis Jackson. He observes that Marty Marion was overrated, that Ozzie Smith just makes a lot of simple plays look spectacular. His idea of a great modern shortstop is Alfredo Griffin. At third base he has Red Rolfe, and Mike Schmidt doesn't even draw a mention, for which I suppose we should be thankful. By the way, did you know that Willie Mays couldn't hit in the clutch? With this record of shrewd talent judgment, it hardly comes as a surprise when Bartell, toward the end of the book, gets a shot as a minor league manager and is a dismal failure. When Bartell is fired as a manager, he is replaced by his second baseman, a 26-year-old named Earl Weaver. The funny part is that Bartell still thinks they made the move to save his salary.

But when the book is good, it can be very good. I find little to fault and much to admire in the writing of the book, which is essentially straightforward. Although Bartell could be a Hall of Famer, Macht and Bartell have the sense not to turn the book into a campaign for his election. The production quality of the book is superb. The book contains only a few typos and an acceptable number of deviations from the historical record. Bartell does not seem to be very bright or very likeable, but he is interesting. It is most worthwhile to make a record of his baseball life. This book is not the product of an economic formula, but of an earnest desire to produce something worthwhile and enjoyable. A note on the dust jacket says that Macht is at work on a biography of Connie Mack. On the one hand, this seems wise, for Macht never really slips into the role of invisible collaborator. In working with a subject from the past he will not have to wrestle that one again. While I am happy for him, there are still a lot of players of the age and quality of Bartell whose stories need to be told. I look forward to the biography of Mack, and to more attempts to tell the stories of players who have been left behind by the spotlight.

JOHN G. CLARKSON (League).

Great Flavor, Weak History

by Len Levin

BLACKBALL STARS: NEGRO LEAGUE PIONEERS
By John B. Holway
Westport, CT: Meckler Books, 1988. $22.50

BASEBALL HISTORIANS, like all other historians, must use true historical method or their conclusions won't stand up under scrutiny. They have to avoid illogic, the sweeping generalization, the vague statistic, the fabulous anecdote — things with which *Blackball Stars* abounds.

For that reason, it would be tempting to make light of this book, which is more or less a sequel to *Voices From the Great Black Baseball Leagues*, John Holway's earlier book on what Holway calls, with obvious double entendre, the blackball stars.

But *Blackball Stars* is still worth reading — indeed a valuable book — if only to open the eyes of its audience (which undoubtedly will be over-whelmingly white) to the realization that before Jackie Robinson there were many great black ballplayers (maybe not as many and as great as Holway contends, but there anyway.)

Most of the two dozen profiles of black players and executives have already been in print, many of them in *SABR Research Journal* or *The National Pastime*. So the most interesting and provocative chapter for SABR members may be the introduction, in which Holway attempts to make a case for greatness of the best Negro League players by pointing to their performance against the best white players. Searches through newspaper files have uncovered 436 games in which blacks played against white major leaguers; of these, he says, the blacks won 268, the white, 168.

How account for these "revolutionary numbers"? Holway seeks to deflect the first answer that comes to mind (to a white mind, anyway): that the whites weren't trying. "The most quoted excuse," he writes, is that the whites were loafing and skylarking and not really trying hard, while the blacks had something to prove; that the whites were just fooling around while the blacks were trying to win. "Yet the image of Cobb stomping off the field after being thrown out by a black catcher and of John McGraw shouting at his New York Giants after losing to a Cuban team dispel this easy explanation." Perhaps, but slim evidence on which to base a historical truth.

Holway concedes that many of the

statistics are incomplete or tentative; the records are still being researched (for that, we owe him and his fellow researchers, both in and out of SABR, a vote of thanks.)

But even if the statistics were more complete, black and white professionals played each other too seldom to provide a valid statistical sample. And you have to read the Negro League statistics with the realization that the black stars were competing against fellow blacks, on fields and with equipment of dubious quality. (If racial integration had come to baseball just two decades earlier, in the 1920s, the picture would have been far more exact, but baseball history is no easier to dig out than any other history.)

Still, there's a lot of meaty reading in *Blackball Stars*, especially if you can overcome Holway's habit of assuming that you, the reader, know as much about black baseball as he and his fellow specialists do, which leads him to be somewhat too casual in identifying teams, leagues, years, etc.

You'll discover, for instance, that though Satchel Paige was more famous, especially among whites, most black ballplayers considered Bullet Joe Rogan, his predecessor as Kansas City Monarchs' mound star, to have been the better pitcher. Paige had the better press and a "white" career, and this illustrates another of the difficulties in coming up with the historic truth about the black players: Our perception of them is largely through the white media, which except for just a few name players, paid practically no attention to the Negro Leagues. To most whites, Paige probably epitomized black baseball; to these same whites, Rogan was unknown.

And while Josh Gibson, one of the 11 Negro Leaguers elected to Cooperstown, is assumed by whites to have been the best of the Negro League catchers, many of his contemporaries thought Louis Santop was a better hitter and thrower, and that Biz Mackey was the best overall — indeed, perhaps the best black player ever (he also played the infield and pitched).

Judy Johnson and Ray Dandridge are in the Hall of Fame as "representatives" of the best black third basemen. But most observers — indeed, Johnson himself — thought Oliver Marcelle was the best at the hot corner.

The fragile structure of the Negro Leagues — financially strapped franchises shifted often and players exercised a degree of mobility that pre-free agency major leaguers might have drooled over — makes it difficult to follow the leagues' history with any degree of exactness. It's best to concentrate on the players, not the teams.

Holway can't resist the tendency to toss facts and figures around like a maladjusted pitching machine. It's hard to digest them all without frequently turning back to an earlier page. So you shouldn't read too much of *Blackball Stars* at one sitting. And read it not for its statistics but for its flavor.

If you do that, you can't help but realize that there's still a big chunk of baseball history out there that remains to be fully documented (Holway and his cohorts could undoubtedly use all the research help they can get).

But, with what information is available so far, trying to "prove" by incomplete and often dubious statistics that *these* guys were better than *those* guys doesn't seem to be the way to do it.

For the Well-Red Only

By Joe Dobrow

**CINCINNATI SEASONS: MY 34 YEARS
WITH THE REDS,** by Earl Lawson
South Bend, IN: Diamond Communications, 1987. $16.95

SOMETIMES YOU DON'T need to read beyond the title of a book to learn virtually everything there is to know about it; and, unfortunately for Cincinnati Reds fans and baseball literati everywhere, this is exactly the case with Earl Lawson's autobigraphical remembrance, *Cincinnati Seasons: My 34 Years with the Reds*. It is a simple account of one reporter's experiences writing about a baseball team -- and, alas, no more.

Lawson, the venerable and sometimes pugnacious baseball writer for the *Cincinnati Post*, made a career of covering the Reds. Beginning in 1950, Lawson followed baseball's oldest team from the foundering days of spring training on through the hot summers and (occasionally) the exciting falls. He was there when Ted Kluszewski cut off his shirt sleeves; there when Johnny Temple roamed second base and when Frank Robinson slugged his way to all kinds of awards; there during the gruff Fred Hutchinson era, and during the transition from Crosley Field to Riverfront Stadium; there during the Glory Years of the 1970s; there, in fact, all the way up until 1984, when the team's fortunes had bottomed out somewhere near the low water mark on the Ohio River.

Lawson was one of the old boy writers, a stiff-jawed, quick-witted Underwood-toting hack in the finest tradition of Red Smith, Jimmy Cannon and Shirley Povich. He didn't just *cover* baseball; he *lived* it. And, mostly in anecdotal snippets, he recounts the charming curiosities of old world baseball beat writer life -- things like friendships formed in late night bars, travel by sleeper car trains, and radio announcers in sweltering press boxes calling games clad only in their undershorts. No doubt Lawson could have gone into even more sordid detail about the players and the writers and the life on the road, but his Midwestern modesty held him back.

But while *Cincinnati Seasons* is sometimes evocative of vivid baseball imagery, this is probably less attributable to Lawson than to baseball itself. Who can't envision in the mind's eye the simple geometry of the diamond, the sideways glance of the pitcher holding a runner on, or the casual bubblegum-blowing look of an on-deck batter swinging two bats with donuts on the end? In Lawson's heyday, the ability to capture such images in writing ("Maloney threw both hands in the air as...the bench emptied onto the field and within a matter of seconds [he] was engulfed by the flailing arms of his teammates") was quite a skill; but in our TV-crazy cable-come-lately age, the need for such writing has disappeared. Consequently, it is tired and, sad to say, redundant.

Still worse, *Cincinnati Seasons* leaves the reader empty and feeling cheated, because Lawson fails where so many journalists-who-would-be-authors before him have failed: he never adapts his episodic, journalistic style to the longer and more thorough work at hand. The result is a piecemeal collection of anecdotes which seem to be arbitrarily broken into sections and chapters with very little thought as to structure or theme. As one old saying goes, "It's tough to edit an editor."

The fanatical Reds rooter can and will forgive Lawson for these shortcomings; he is, after all (as he is quick to point out), a part of the baseball scene in Cincinnati. What cannot be forgiven, though, is the disappointingly brief treatment he gives to the Glory Years. Except for a few shill pieces (e.g. - The Relentless Reds, The Main Spark), no work has been written that adequately captures the excitement and euphoria of the 1970s, when the Reds were baseball's best team. With this book, Lawson had the chance. But unfortunately, except for one brief chapter and a couple of fairly simplistic personality profiles -- again, in his squeaky clean anecdotal style -- he pays only passing tribute to Rose, Bench, Anderson and the rest of the Big Red Machine. Perhaps it was a conscious choice on Lawson's part to downplay the modern and obvious, and accentuate the ancient and obscure, but given the audience attracted to this book, it was a poor choice.

Ultimately, the biggest disappointment is in the discovery that *My 34 Years with the Reds* is not just "34 Years with the Reds." It is the story of Lawson more than of the team, and quite frankly, he is not as interesting as the players and games he covered. We simply are not that keen to hear why he got slugged by Johnny Temple, or why he took Vada Pinson to court. We would rather hear more about the train rides and the announcers in shorts and the great Game of yesteryear, to which he was eyewitness.

While there may be a place for this sort of autobiographical history, this is not it. Lawson did not realize this when he set out to write the book, or when he gave it a title. His closing is not some sort of elegiac exclamation point to his own career, but instead a rather anemic roster run-down of the current Reds (including a line about the immortal Terry McGriff), and the milquetoast conclusion that "One thing's for sure -- there are many exciting Cincinnati seasons yet to come!" Thanks, Earl, for that stunning revelation.

In short, *Cincinnati Seasons* is a mildly entertaining and lightweight work which holds few surprises. As was the case with Red Smith, a more significant book would be a collection of his columns and articles through the years. Perhaps when that comes out, there will be something worth digesting beyond the title.

O'Malley As A Visionary

By Pete Cava

THE DODGERS MOVE WEST, by Neil J. Sullivan
New York: Oxford University Press, 1987. $17.95

BY APRIL OF 1958 THE Brooklyn Dodgers had forsaken Ebbets Field for California. But it wasn't until June of that year that the team's future in Los Angeles — which would eventually reap attendance harvests of more than three million customers - was ensured.

Neil Sullivan's *The Dodgers Move West* deftly chronicles the uprooting of what many considered to be the original "America's Team."

June 4, 1958, marks the date when the voters of Los Angeles approved an agreement to provide the land at Chavez Ravine for the Dodgers' future home. A trivial fact, no doubt, but there's nothing trivial about Sullivan's effort.

True, the book is about much more than baseball. Sullivan astutely plumbs the political meanderings on two coasts that brought about the move.

One of the favorite theories concerning the Dodgers' move — certainly one of the most controversial franchise shifts, and one that broke the heart on an entire borough — is the ruthlessness of Walter O'Malley, the team's chief executive.

Sullivan treats the O'Malley Devil Theory — expounded by Peter Golenbock, Roger Kahn and others — as a shibboleth. "O'Malley's crime was to remove the fig leaf from baseball," writes Sullivan. "He openly considered displayed what others had camouflaged in rhetoric. Thus, while his peers — Rickey, MacPhail, and George Weiss — have been elected to the Hall of Fame, even the suggestion that O'Malley belongs there would inspire fierce controversy."

Sullivan dismisses O'Malley as a mere minor leaguer when compared with the politicos in New York and Los Angeles whose frequently unscrupulous behavior determined the team's fate.

Sullivan's research on the subject is commendable. He has rendered an accurate portrayal of the early transformation of sport to business...a transformation that has plagued the purists during the second half of this century.

Perhaps the book's only flaw is Sullivan's attempt to justify the Dodgers' shift. Sure, it reaped tremendous profits. And O'Malley was a businessman, as everyone who has survived the age of Finley, Turner and Steinbrenner can attest to.

In the book's final chapter, Sullivan

notes: "The history of the Dodgers in both Brooklyn and Los Angeles demonstrates that the romance of baseball is universal. The emotional attachments a community may feel for a team are insufficient to ensure that the franchise will remain where it is beloved. Major league teams will always be a scarce commodity, and cities will inevitably compete for a limited number of teams. Disappointment and even bitterness will accompany the allocation of franchises."

True enough. But my love for baseball was formed in New York in that city's final era as a three-team town. And I remember the sad impact this move west had on my Dodger-loving schoolmates. For them the loss of the Dodgers was as devastating as the end of an eighth grade love affair; as painful as the death of a beloved pet. Even a confirmed Dodger-hating Yankee fan could sympathize.

And for this reason, I always feel a secret joy anytime the Dodgers lose.

Sullivan's apologia excepted, *The Dodgers Move West* rates a "can't-miss" tag.

BASE-BALL—FOR THE SPECTATOR.

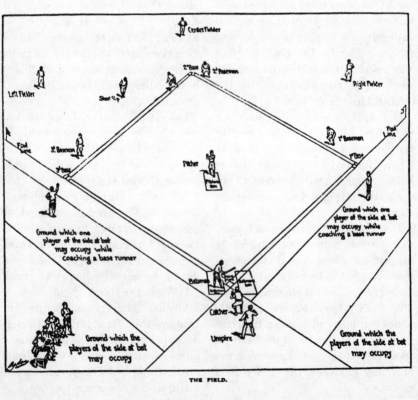

THE FIELD.

The Team You Love-- Or Love to Hate

by Paul Adomites

THE NEW YORK METS: TWENTY-FIVE YEARS OF BASEBALL MAGIC
By Jack Lang and Peter Simon
New York: Henry Holt and Company, 1987. $13.95

IN TWENTY-FIVE YEARS, THE Mets have changed face completely: from the world's most lovable losers to its most despised champions. It's almost as if their remarkable arrogance today is somehow the mirror image of the buffoon hat they wore at the beginning; both are more cartoon-like than real, both have little to do with the playing of baseball.

Jack Lang, estimable Secretary-Treasurer of the Baseball Writers' Association of America, has combined with photographer Peter Simon to write the history of this team, the team that, no matter what else, has always been "Amazing."

Unlike most team histories, this one doesn't have to search into a deep dark past; the Mets weren't invented until 1962. And Lang covered them as a beat reporter for most of their history. The result is a perspective on a team that almost no one else could have. And that is the crowning strength of this book.

It is complete. In some ways it can serve as a model for all team histories that follow. It lists the Neft and Cohen stats and the opening day lineup for every year, *plus* the Mets' first pick in every June free agent draft, every Mets' grand slam, no-hitter, Gold Glove winner (six total, Hernandez three), Rusty Staub's pinch hits, most pitching wins *against* the Mets, All-Star Game selections, hitting streaks, one-hitters, the team record in one-run games, etc. And that's just the marginalia.

Lang tells a clear story of how the team came to be, developed the great pitching that led it to a World Championship in just its eighth year, how the ownership led it back into mediocrity, and then how new owners (the chapter is called "Doubleday to the Rescue") changed direction again. Originally published to celebrate the Mets' twenty-fifth year, a chapter was added to update through the World Series championship of 1986.

Along the way, Lang doesn't miss a trick. He captures the change of heart that made Casey Stengel expendable. He takes credit for introducing Stengel to Westrum, his successor. He covers in detail all those *long* games the Mets have played. (Is it just me, or do they always play longer than most?) The politicking at the top: the internecine squabbles between Strawberry and the gang; it's all here. If you want to know how much the Mets spent on their 1986 pre-World Series party, this is where to look.

You'll find your favorite Met characters here, too. Wes Westrum's ability to out-Yogi the master: "Boy that was a real cliffdweller!" Tug and Swoboda, Choo Choo, Seaver and Mazzilli. Who could forget Lenny Randle?

Lang touches briefly on the team's *character*, singular. Why so many fights? Howard Johnson's response, "They can't beat us on the field, so they try to beat us up," is so consistent with the Mets' attitude that it gives the reason without saying it. (My favorite Mets' move is the whiny face, perfected by Gary Carter, but imitated by many, when a call goes against them. I swear I have seen Mr. Carter stare at the home plate umpire with his adolescent pout after *swinging* at the third strike.)

There are lots of great photos, too. Willie Mays in tears during his "night" at Shea. Disheveled Tom Seaver and Gary Gentry survey the damage the lovable Mets fans caused to the field after the 1969 World Series. A four-photo panel covers the Harrelson-Rose battle during the 1973 playoffs.

This book isn't perfect. Some of the lapses are excusable. Claiming that Dwight Gooden has "practically re-written the record book for pitching feats" is New York-style hype. Those of us in the hinterlands are quite used to it. I'm still puzzling over the opening sentence to chapter seventeen: "Joe MacDonald and Joe Frazier were an entry."

But the biggest problem is organizational. The chapters are not simply year-by-year, which is fine (some years barely rate mention in the Mets' life, or in mine, for that matter). But it's easy to get the feeling that Mr. Lang's outline was printed, and then they told him to go back and "beef it up." A transition is stated, you get the message, then the book goes backward in time. For example, "The Mets came home from California to take on St. Louis in a three-game series starting September 10." Don't you expect the next thing you read will be about that series? After all, the Mets "came home." But not here. Instead we get an eleven-paragraph description of the road trip they "came home" from. The effect is unsettling.

Overall, this book is much less story-telling than it is fact-relating. Which makes it less than thrilling to read, but more valuable for research. And as a research vehicle, as I said above, it is complete, accurate, and enjoyable. The next time you sit down to write a team history, start by studying this one.

Intelligence and Ambition At Work

By George Robinson

GETTING BLUE by Peter Gethers
New York: Delacorte, 1987. $16.95

ONE OF THE MAJOR attractions of baseball is its leisurely pace. Basketball is a non-stop tumult of action, football, an explosion every minute or so. In baseball, events come slowly, giving one time to contemplate. The best baseball fiction, I think, partakes of those same languid rhythms. (Perhaps that is why I find W.P. Kinsella's novels, with their *longeurs* that drive so many readers up the wall, so satisfying.)

Peter Gethers, the author of *Getting Blue*, should be well aware of those rhythms. He is one of the founders of the original Rotisserie League and an avid baseball fan. However, *Getting Blue* is one of those baseball novels that isn't really about baseball at all. Mind you, there is absolutely nothing wrong with that. This is probably not the best forum in which to express this thought, but there are many more important things in life than baseball.

Getting Blue traces the emotional evolution of Alex Justin, a ballplayer, from his youth as a top high school prospect in New York in the 1950s through a promising beginning in the low minors to a mysterious descent to journeyman status in the majors, a brief golden moment in his one and only World Series appearance, and a dissolute, depressed retirement. Along the way, Gethers throws in jazz, corporate corruption, racism, wife beating, infidelity, a little covert zen philosophizing, sex and a lot of death and despair.

Gethers's problem lies in the way in which he piles events on top of one another, basketball or football fashion. Consider this sequence of events: in successive chapters, 1) minor leaguer Alex makes it with a local waitress, betraying his high school love back home, engendering several chapters worth of guilt in the process; 2) his best friend on the team, a black player, is attacked, his tongue cut out by Klan-types; 3) Alex's roommate is rendered a vegetable in a beaning incident. When events are piled up this way what results is either melodrama or farce. I wish Gethers were trying for farce; in its sheer excess, this material cries out for it.

Gethers's hero, Alex Justin, is a man from whom everything is taken. His parents are killed in a plane crash. His brother and childhood friend betray him in business. His marriage falls apart. His son commits suicide while he looks on helplessly. All that Gethers leaves him is his friendship with his ex-wife and with a man who is a national outcast for abandoning baseball, and his endless quest for self-knowledge.

Alex has spent his whole life searching for The Moment, as he calls it, a perfect moment on the field. He seeks what Sam Shepard once described as "a true gesture that won't never cheat on itself 'cause it's the last of its kind." The irony, of course, is that such a gesture is virtually impossible in baseball, because as Earl Weaver says, "we gotta do this again tomorrow." There's always another game. Alex will wake up one morning, out of baseball and at a loss for meaning. (In fact, the best part of the book is Alex's coping with retirement, not the melodramatic hogwash of betrayal and suicide, but the mundane stuff of daily existence away from the spotlight.)

Alex's quest is at the heart of the book, and is its biggest problem. So much of this book is spent in idle, banal philosophizing, with Alex, an eternal innocent even at his most dissolute, trying to find what it all means. Because Alex is so secretive—no one knows of the quest for The Moment—much of the book is taken up with his ruminations on these questions of existence. After a promising opening in Central Park, *Getting Blue* turns into a restless, often pointless, alternation between melodramatic incident and aimless discussion of same.

And yet there is something there. Gethers has written a novel that fails messily, but it is a failure of intelligence and ambition. There are flashes of inspiration here—the use of jazz as an extended metaphor comparable to baseball, Gethers's feel for the horseplay of ballplayers in a small town, some of the humor, especially a brief scene in which Patty, Alex's ex-wife, walks in on him masturbating. Peter Gethers is simply too smart not to write a better book than this. On some level, *Getting Blue*'s sheer ambition muddles it. It reminds me of advice I give my students: limit yourself to one idea per sentence.

This Spitball Is Loaded With Poetry

by Gerald Tomlinson

EXACTLY A HUNDRED YEARS AGO, ON JUNE 3, 1888, Ernest Lawrence Thayer's "Casey at the Bat" appeared in the *San Francisco Examiner*. Baseball and the written word have been on good terms ever since. It was not until 1981, however, that the game acquired a literary journal all its own, *Spitball*, a small, unpretentious quarterly founded by Mike Shannon, who now directs it, and the late W.J. (Jim) Harrison of Covington, Kentucky. The magazine entered the literary field with the avowed purpose of publishing baseball poetry. In the eight years since then, for 26 issues to date, it has successfully done that, and much more.

To begin with what filmmakers call an establishing shot, *Spitball* is a 5½ by 8½ inch paperback magazine, saddlestitched (i.e., stapled), issued four times a year--March, June, September, December--and featuring, in addition to poetry, a lively mix of short fiction, articles, interviews, book reviews, line drawings, and, albeit rarely, photographs. The text appears in typewriter type just as SABR's *Baseball Research Journal* did in its formative years. The first issue of *Spitball* consisted of 20 pages; recent ones contain 52 pages.

From the outset, the magazine has sponsored two annual literary contests: one for baseball poetry, the other for baseball fiction. The prizes, as with most small literary magazines, are basically just free copies of the magazine. Its biggest one-time competitive event to date, the centennial "Casey at the Bat" Poetry Contest, gained some publicity around the country and brought forth the varied efforts that dominate issue #26, June 1988.

Beginning with a tribute to Johnny Bench in issue #8 (all issues will hereafter be referred to by number), *Spitball* has occasionally focused on an individual player or on a particular aspect of baseball. Issue #15, for example, features Pete Rose; #21, ballparks; and #24, blacks in baseball.

Spitball sponsors one big annual affair, the Casey Awards Banquet, held in January at the Carnegie Arts Center in Covington, Kentucky, across the river from Cincinnati, where the magazine is published. The Casey is a bronze plaque ("very beautiful and expensive to make") given to both the author and the publisher of the year's best baseball book, as chosen by a panel of three judges: Eric Rolfe Greenberg's novel *The Celebrant* won the first Casey in 1983. Subsequent winners: Peter Golenbock's *Bums* (1984); Roger Kahn's *Good Enough to Dream* (1985); Bill James's *The Bill James Historical Baseball Abstract* (1986); and *Diamonds Are Forever*, edited by Peter H. Gordon, Sydney Waller, and Paul Weinman (1987).

This January a crowd converged on the Carnegie Arts Center for *Spitball*'s 1988 Casey conclave, including, as always, a few nominated authors, among them David Voigt and Paul Weinman. The banquet, like the magazine itself, has been growing and improving year by year. It has become literary baseball's equivalent of SABR's annual convention.

The man behind this shoestring-to-bootstrap venture, *Spitball*'s publisher and editor, Mike Shannon (no relation to "Moonman," the one-time journeyman St. Louis Cardinal), notes that the magazine "is definitely in the tradition of the small poetry/literary magazine (those that are labors of love)." With virtually no advertising budget Shannon has found it hard to reach the larger audience he believes must exist. Now and then, however, free publicity comes his way. On February 4, 1987, *The Wall Street Journal* carried a front-page article by Jolie Solomon, "Baseball Is a Game Of Hits, Runs, Errors And Lyric Poetry," that describes *Spitball* at length and, on the whole, very favorably. The magazine, Solomon writes, is "dedicated to those whose passion for the game of inches is equaled only by their passion for the well-chosen word."

This spring Pocket Books brought out a handsome paperback book, *The Best of Spitball*, edited by--who else?--Mike Shannon. *The Best of Spitball* is a 173-page anthology and an ideal introduction to the magazine. Readers who like the anthology selections will like *Spitball*.

Literary magazines are chancy propositions at best, and few who saw the premier issue of *Spitball* (Spring 1981) would have predicted a bright future for the Shannon-Harrison enterprise. Among the best of its 13 poems is Arthur Mann Kaye's "One Thinks of Willie Mays," but, alas for newness, it had already appeared in Roger Angell's *The Summer Game*. The most noteworthy original poem is editor Mike Shannon's own "The Mantle-Mays Controversy Solved." No short stories appear in the premier issue. One curious inclusion is Terry Smith's nonfiction piece, "1946: Bill Kennedy's Fabulous Year," which prompts a question that arises insistently later on: Does even the most sweeping definition of literature include such workaday prose as this excerpt from Smith's privately published book about baseball in Rocky Mount, North Carolina?

Mike Shannon's choice for the best issue to date is #22, published in June 1987. And no wonder. From Darryl Lankford's classy cover drawing of a caricatured W.P. Kinsella in a cornfield to the book reviews at the end of the magazine, issue #22 is a delight. Fine baseball fiction by Jim Brosnan, Eugene C. Flinn, and cover-subject Kinsella, along with a revealing *Spitball* interview with Kinsella (author of the novel *Shoeless Joe*) make up most of the issue. Brosnan's "Hardball, Aunt Steve, and the White Sox," which leads off, is a charming tale of youthful fandom. Flinn's "Never Mind 'Who's on First?' Who's in the Outfield?" is a fantasy about an aficionado's wife, the redoubtable Patti, who sets Whitey Herzog's fading Cardinals straight with "good molecules." Kinsella's "Diehard" uses the old ashes-scattered-on-the-ball-field theme in a light-hearted but touching way.

Concerning issue #22, Shannon remarks that "we usually have a better mix of poetry and fiction...in a typical general issue we have a little more poetry (in terms of numbers of pages) than fiction, but we always like to have at least one short story (usually about 10 pages in length)." In that sense, then, #22 isn't a model issue--but in most other senses it is. A sizable portion of issue #22 made its way into *The Best of Spitball*.

Although #22 with its short stories is the best single issue, the truth is that *Spitball*'s greatest strength is, as originally envisioned, its poetry. Except for parodies, the poems are nearly all written in free verse, a somewhat limiting form, paradoxically, since it lends a stylistic similarity to much of the poetry. Among the best of the poems are Mike Shannon's "The Last Days of Forbes Field: A Nightmare" (#4), Tom Sheehan's "In Cold Fields" (#6), James Perkins's "Pop Foul/Crosley Field, 1949" (#14), Robert J. Harrison's "The Answer from Alex Weissman at the Asylum for the Insane, Rockland County, New York" (#21), and Tim Peeler's "Niekro Summoning Paige" (#24).

Nancy Breen's "Devotion" (#8) is appealing except for a single image-- "her hands two snoozing/doves"--that doesn't connect. Jim Palana's "Baker Bowl--Philadelphia" (#21) is marvelous all the way to the last line--" ...baseball when the grass was real." Shades of Joe Biden. It's a good line all right, but it's not a Palana original.

Gene Fehler has published more poems in *Spitball* than any other contributor. His poems include a number of parodies, the best of which is "Baseball Manager: Five Variations on William Carlos Williams' 'This Is Just to Say' " (#7). The problem with most of his and others' parodies in issues #7 and #10 is that they aren't very funny. Some show evidence of being purposely serious--an odd aim for a parody.

Nonetheless, poetry is the forte of *Spitball*, and, like the magazine itself, the poems, on the whole, are getting better with each issue.

So is the short fiction, which rose to Brosnan-Flinn-Kinsella heights in issue #22. What has been done once can presumably be done again. Prior to #22, however, the short stories fall well short of the poetry. Fantasy seems to be the preferred mode, with golden-age superstars whimsically and sometimes irritatingly rewriting what SABRites have always supposed to be baseball history. An exception is Bill Howard's "The Charlie Pepper Letters" (#16), which is anything but a fantasy. Indeed, it is a rather grisly tale that might have been, and perhaps was, constructed from newspaper accounts of Cincinnati catcher Willard Hershberger's suicide in 1940. It's engrossing, but no more so than James Barbour's factual "The Death of Willard Hershberger" in *The National Pastime* (Winter 1987).

Three of the best *Spitball* stories besides those in #22 are an early Kinsella effort, "How I Got My Nickname" (#8); Daniel McAfee's "Batting 1.000" (#20); and Dallas Wiebe's "The Measure Thereof Shall Be After the Homer" (#23). In general, though, *Spitball*'s short fiction has some catching up to do in comparison with its poetry.

Nonfiction raises a fundamental issue that was evident in issue #1. There aren't a whole lot of essays (that is to say, articles) in *Spitball*, and the ones that do appear can hardly be called belletristic. On literary merit alone, nothing published so far in "The Literary Baseball Magazine" could not more logically have appeared in SABR's *Baseball Research Journal*. Admirable short baseball nonfiction does exist, as witness the Einstein *Fireside* books, the Thorn *Armchair* books, and *The National Pastime* (all of which contain a sampling of fiction and poetry as well), but superior nonfiction has yet to make its way, at least in the form of original submissions, to Mike Shannon's office. Should *Spitball* include nonfiction? Why not, if the quality of the writing warrants it? Shannon would be delighted, no doubt, to offer a prose piece on the order of John Updike's "Hub Fans Bid Kid Adieu," an unforgettable sketch of Ted Williams's last game that first appeared in *The New Yorker*. The difficulty lies in finding one or more undiscovered John Updikes.

This is not to say that there is no worthwhile nonfiction in *Spitball*. Dick Miller's essay "Old Crosley" (#21), a nostalgic look at the Cincinnati Reds' former ballpark, is a solid effort. And Mike Shannon's "Suspicions, Surprises, and Speeches: Induction Weekend '87" (#23) is an engaging personal look at the Baseball Hall of Fame ceremonies in which Ray Dandridge, Catfish Hunter, and Billy Williams were inducted. Shannon spent that Saturday on a Cooperstown street corner passing out free Catfish Hunter commemorative poem cards that he had had printed--an attractive souvenir as well as a not-so-subtle advertisement for *Spitball*. The reaction of the passing throng did not always warm the heart of the poet-publisher. "It seemed that the only thing more foreign to them than the idea of a poem," he reported, "was the idea of a poem about a baseball player." Still, he gave out more than 800 cards, and some people even said, "Thanks."

The first *Spitball* interview appeared in issue #5, a conversation with Gene Fehler, who in the early days of the magazine was a regular contributor of both poems and fiction. Subsequent interviews with National Baseball Hall of Fame librarian Tom Heitz (#10), player-author Jim Brosnan (#14), biographer Charles C. Alexander (#15), and others have established the interview as a valuable feature, one that has surely earned a place in the future of the magazine. Although *Spitball* is hardly a how-to publication, the fact is that interviews with established writers can be fascinating and highly valuable to other writers—and it's a safe bet that most of *Spitball* subscribers have a few manuscripts tucked away in their desk drawers.

Book reviews surfaced in *Spitball* just one issue ahead of interviews (in issue #4). Unlike the interviews, the book reviews have occasionally gotten out of hand—in issue #17, for example, which devotes 22 of its 40 pages to them. That proportion might be all right if all or most of the books reviewed had at least a vague claim (other than having been set in type) to being called baseball literature. They don't. Why, for instance, would anyone expect to, or want to, read about Gary Matthews's *They Call Me Sarge* in a literary magazine? One has to wonder from this issue what the criteria are for a book to be reviewed in *Spitball*. While W.P. Kinsella's *The Thrill of the Grass*, a baseball short-story collection, surely deserves a long and thoughtful review (which it gets from the versatile Mike Shannon), it's not clear that Harvey Frommer's *Baseball's Greatest Managers* qualifies for half a page of attention in the magazine. It isn't literature, nor does it pretend to be. Better a half-page "retrospective review" of a book, however old, of at least passing literary interest, such as Zane Grey's *The Red Headed Outfielder and Other Baseball Stories* (1920), or Douglas Wallop's *The Year the Yankees Lost the Pennant* (1954), or Paul Hemphill's *Long Gone* (1979). Even poor current baseball fiction would seem to merit review space in *Spitball*, while all but the best nonfiction—Roger Kahn's *Good Enough to Dream*, perhaps, although my own assessment of Kahn's book is less fulsome than *Spitball*'s—has a more tenuous claim on the magazine's limited space.

No adverse criticism of the actual reviews is intended. There are some good ones. Among *Spitball*'s able reviewers are Kevin Grace, not surprisingly since he's the magazine's Book Review Editor, and Bill Vernon, whose review of Daniel Okrent's *Nine Innings* (#15) is a model of the genre, although Vernon's ultimate judgment on the book differs from that of Jeffrey Neuman in the Premier Issue of *The SABR Review of Books*. (Vernon likes the book, Neuman doesn't.)

Spitball is still a relatively new magazine. It's in the process of defining, or perhaps refining, itself. As Luke Salisbury wonders in *The SABR Review of Books*, Volume II, "Why Is It So Hard to Write a Good Baseball Novel?" Mike Shannon must often have wondered what elements make up an ideal literary baseball magazine. He comes closer to a cogent answer with his later issues than with the earlier ones, but some difficulties persist.

The overriding difficulty is one of definition. What, exactly, is baseball literature? It's true that many of the heavy hitters in America's recent literary lineup have penned something about baseball. William Carlos Williams, Marianne Moore, and Donald Hall have written baseball poems. Carl Sandburg's "Notes for a Preface" in his *Complete Poems* begins with two baseball anecdotes, one about Babe Ruth, the other about Ty Cobb. Yet the world's best-known baseball poem, Ernest Lawrence Thayer's "Casey at the Bat," is, in all honesty (and much as we may love it), essentially comic verse. *[Note: Glenn Stout feels otherwise. See page 7.]* The same is true of Franklin P. Adams's "Baseball's Sad Lexicon," which assured Tinker, Evers, and Chance of quotable immortality, but didn't elevate poet-columnist FPA to Westminster Abbey's Poets' Corner.

Spitball's only direct involvement with the baseball novel is as a reviewer, not a publisher. What Mike Shannon needs for his magazine is an influx of good baseball short stories. Unfortunately, good baseball short stories are hard to come by, because their writers face the same dilemmas as baseball novelists. Realistic short fiction is an all but pointless exercise—baseball has plenty of drama without the aid of play-by-play contrivance. Fantasy, like poetry, appeals to romantics, but it can drive literal-minded fans to the real-life excitement of TV's Sports Channel. Stories in which one or more of the main characters are famous major league ballplayers, manipulated like puppets in the author's febrile brain, can make knowledgeable fans wish that E. L. Doctorow had lost his *Ragtime* manuscript on the way to the publisher. Ring Lardner's "Alibi Ike" and James Thurber's "You Could Look It Up" are perhaps the most widely known baseball short stories, at least by title, and, like "Casey at the Bat," they're humorous. Maybe there's a moral here. Could it be that, since baseball is a game, humor is the perfect imaginative medium for it? Certainly, the most impressive short stories in *Spitball* up to now have had a humorous slant. So, too, have a few of the best poems.

Seriousness in itself is not a fault, of course, but the hagiography in *Spitball* sometimes is. Men and women who are inspired to produce baseball poetry or fiction have their revered heroes, as we all do, and occasionally these writers have an irrestible impulse to pen tributes to their paladins. Judging by a few (though decidedly not all) of the odes in *Spitball*, writers should resist, or at least question, the urge. Ernie Banks is not Ulysses; Babe Ruth is not Zeus. Most of the best serious poetry in the magazine deals with baseball not canonically or mythologically, but abstractly or peripherally. The best poetry, like the best fiction, is devoid of both play-by-play realism and hero-worshipping sentimentality. Tom Sheehan's "In Cold Fields," to take a single example, could almost be classified as a war poem rather than a baseball poem. Its ballplayers are kids, not professionals, and the real game they're learning concerns life, as young "Billy centerfield" can testify, having left "his arm/in Kwajalein debris." It's a far cry from apotheosizing yet another superstar.

A few general thoughts about *Spitball*: The idea of honoring the best baseball book of the year is a good one, but it's doubtful that any panel of judges can make a rational choice between a surrealistic novel, let's say, and a book like *The Bill James Historical Baseball Abstract*. Or between Mike Shannon's tiny chapbook, *Pete Rose Agonistes* (if that were to be nominated), and David L. Porter's monumental *Biographical Dictionary of American Sports: Baseball* (ditto). The Casey Award, to be meaningful, should compare apples with apples, oranges with oranges. If there's to be only one Casey each year, the competition should probably be restricted to fiction. Granted, such a change would impose severe limitations—in some years there might be no winner—but it would also add meaning to the award. Better yet, if two broad categories were to be established, fiction and nonfiction, there would always be at least one annual award, the one in the nonfiction category.

A *Spitball* reader has to know his or her baseball much better than the average bleacher creature. Up to a point that's fine. No one but a dedicated baseball fan is going to read the magazine anyway. But even a dedicated fan may sometimes be confused by the lack of explanatory headnotes or accompanying text. For example, Jim Palana's series of monologues in "The Wall" (#14), intriguing as it is, demands a knowledge of Boston Red Sox history that may be too much to expect of even the most tuned-in *Spitball* reader. In issue #17, Sue Bogyo's cover art draws a "Wow! Pretty good, wouldn't you say!" Well, yes, but who *are* those three players pictured? (It turns out that they're the 1987 Hall of Fame inductees, Ray Dandridge, Catfish Hunter, and Billy Williams.)

So much for complaints. *Spitball*, on balance, is a clear success. Eight years after its founding, the magazine seems much less a "quixotic venture," in Jim Brosnan's words, than it did at the beginning. A growing body of fine baseball poems and short stories attests to the fact that not all the best baseball writing is factual.

In late 1980, over a few beers and across the Ohio River from River-front Stadium, Cincinnati, Mike Shannon and Jim Harrison had a vision—a vision for a baseball literary magazine, an "unlikely marriage," they thought at the time, but one that was consummated as fully as the mysterious prophesy, "If you build it, he will come," in W.P. Kinsella's *Shoeless Joe*. Shannon and Harrison built *Spitball*, the literary edifice, and an increasing number of talented writers and appreciative readers have been streaming through the gates ever since.

Baseball is inherently artistic. Not every ballplayer down through the years has viewed it that way, of course, but it is. Mike Shannon, his staff, and the contributors to *Spitball* look upon the game as one of America's finer arts, and the literature of baseball has benefited from their percep-tion. Daniel Okrent, author of *The Ultimate Baseball Book*, comments in his blurb for *The Best of Spitball*, "Whenever I need to be reminded of the music of baseball, I read *Spitball*—its best pieces are as true as a shot to the wall."

True enough.

And as lively as a Burleigh Grimes spitter.

Subscription information: Spitball's mailing address is 6224 Collegevue Place, Cincinnati, Ohio 45224. Subscription rates are $10 for one year, $18 for two years, $100 lifetime.

Bats, Balls and Gowns — Academic Dissertations on Baseball Literature, Culture and History

by Peter C. Bjarkman

IF ACADEMIC DISSERTATIONS ON BASEBALL LITERATURE and baseball history provide a fruitful scholarly resource, this is not yet common knowledge among our active baseball researchers. Confirmation of the anonymity surrounding this rich body of work is provided in a curious statement buried within a recent issue of *The SABR Bulletin*. Here we learn from a report of the SABR Microfilm Committee (December 1986) that Edward Nichols' pioneering 1939 Ph.D. thesis (Pennsylvania State University) is "perhaps still the only dissertation on baseball completed in a Department of English at an American university." What is more distressing than the mere inaccuracy of this statement is what it reveals about the relative obscurity still surrounding academic work on baseball history and baseball culture. That such inaccuracies should be fostered by SABR, of all groups, further masks the degree to which baseball has remained a favorite pastime (albeit often a secretive passion) of hundreds of American scholars and academics. More importantly, it works to direct aspiring students of the game away from one of the richest if least-mined veins of information on the early history as well as the literary potential of our fascinating national pastime.

Baseball dissertations, then, remain one of the richest resources for scholarly interpretation of baseball, and yet at the same time one of the least explored sources available to students of baseball history and baseball literature. This report is intended as a guide for those wishing to explore these existing academic resources of our Literary Baseball. "Abstract" summaries are provided below for nineteen readily accessible baseball dissertations on historical and literary topics, all focusing on baseball as a subject in American literary or cultural studies. I have narrowed my survey here to those Ph.D. theses which explore in detail the impact of baseball on American life and American letters; this listing is therefore not exhaustive of all doctoral dissertations which, after one fashion or another, touch either directly or obliquely on baseball as a subject of academic inquiry. This survey is nonetheless hopefully representative of the considerable degree to which American scholars have found baseball and baseball culture a challenging and fascinating subject for scholarly inquiry.

Doctoral dissertations exploring baseball as a literary subject hold considerable significance, then, for scholars of both baseball history and American culture: these works chronicle the emergence of a serious adult baseball fiction and explore various important aspects of this emerging literary genre. Baseball dissertations on historical topics also hold a similar scholarly value: together they provide a body of writings which help explain precisely why a serious baseball literature and fiction develop, as they do, only after 1950. And they record as well the historical background on which that fiction continues to draw for its vital socio-cultural perspectives and for its fertile intellectual life-source. These scholarly works explore precisely why popular baseball themes of "the pastoral," "the non-urban," and "the non-commercial" arise only after the national sport has effectively lost its folk roots and today become largely an urban commercial spectacle.

NOTE:
Below doctoral dissertations awarded at American universities all feature discussion of the role of baseball in American literature, the literary uses of baseball, or the role of baseball in American culture and American social history. Dissertations are divided here into distinct categories -- literary and historical. *DAI* abstract numbers and volume information are provided here to guide the reader in locating full abstracts for each dissertation in the appropriate *DAI* volume. *DAI* is an abbreviation for *Dissertation Abstracts International*, published by University Microfilms International, Ann Arbor, Michigan 48106. End-item volume and page numbers refer here to the location of *DAI* abstract listings, and reference librarians will presumably guide the reader to *DAI* volumes in any major university or public library reference department. Ordering information for purchasing cloth-bound or microfilm copies of individual dissertations can be obtained by phoning 800-521-0600 or 313-761-4700. Phone orders require the *DAI* order number (provided below for each dissertation) as well as author's name and title, and major credit card payments are possible.

1. Dissertations on Baseball in American Literature

Bowles, Francis P. America at Bat: The Baseball Hero in Life and Letters. *Ph.D. Dissertation. The University of New Mexico, 1980 (no DAI catalog listing, abstract or order number; available only through inter-library loan from the University of New Mexico Graduate Library).*

The argument gracefully advanced here is that the game of professional baseball, along with its players, reflects psychological and moral truths about the American national experience. Baseball and the men who play it together "embody the collective drives and aspirations of the larger society around them." This study takes social history as its organizing frame, defining baseball as a central American social institution. From this viewpoint, the "dead-ball" era of the early 20th century as well as the slugging era of the '20s closely mirror national life during these two remarkably different historical periods. Individual chapters focus on a number of important baseball personages who in themselves reflect contemporary American values and issues: Albert Spalding is presented in the perspective of the Horatio Alger novels; Christy Mathewson is seen as a living embodiment of Gilbert Patten's Frank Merriwell image which dominated sporting fiction at the turn of the century; John Montgomery Ward's "Brotherhood Rebellion" provides almost perfect counterpoint to the economic stance of Albert Spalding, just as John McGraw provides an instructive contrast to the conception of the baseball hero created by the fiction of Patten and the on-field play of Mathewson. Following a line of argumentation developed by Tristram Coffin, Bowles demonstrates as well that baseball heroes such as Babe Ruth, Ty Cobb, and Judge Landis complete the normal developmental process of national folklore by personifying expected American types (the ideal prowess hero, the trickster, the ethical figure.) A controversial thesis concerning the position of blacks in American baseball suggests that "because black stars in the major leagues have refused to act out the stereotyped 'Old Coon' role that whites have expected them to play, Satchel Paige is the only Negro star to achieve legendary status" within baseball's national mythology.

Candelaria, Cordelia (Chavez). Baseball in American Literature: From Ritual to Fiction. *Ph.D. Dissertation. University of Notre Dame, 1976 (200 pp).* DAI 37, No. 01, 305-A (Order no. DDJ76-16493).

Explicates the serious adult novel-length prose fiction about baseball produced through the mid-1970s, exclusive of youth baseball novels and other pulp dime-novels devoted to the sport during the earlier half of the present century. Two types of novels are covered: those in which baseball plays only a minor role as one of several competing organization metaphors, and those in which baseball is the controlling and dominant literary figure, one which establishes the novel's controlling themes. A central socio-historical thesis emerges: "baseball fiction as a body shows a progression from the simpler dimensions of romanticism and realism to the more complex ironic and autotelic modes, [and this progression] has a cultural correlative in baseball itself." Paralleling the complex evolution of our baseball fiction is the evolution of the on-field game as well, from native 19th-century folk-ritual to the increasingly sophisticated and commercialized professional endeavor of the twentieth century. An ever-widening distance between ballgame and folk population is seen as distinctly in the literary uses of baseball as it is in the emergence of the spectator sport itself. The shift in baseball fiction from simply structured and simply narrated action-packed stories to acutely solipsistic fictions is demonstrated with works of such recent novelists as Malamud *(The Natural)*, Coover *(The Universal Baseball Association)*, John Alexander Graham *(Babe Ruth Caught in a Snowstorm)*, and Roth *(The Great American Novel)*.

Dagavarian, Debra. A Descriptive Analysis of Baseball Fiction in Children's Periodicals: 1880-1950. *Ed.D. Dissertation. Rutgers University, 1987 (no DAI catalog listing, abstract, or order number; inter-library loan available from Rutgers University Libraries).*

The research purpose here is to explore and describe content from an important American cultural artifact: children's periodical fiction treating the game of baseball. Children's magazine baseball fiction is analyzed in terms of social and historical origins, as well as intended audience, with a controlling assumption that such fiction plays a vital part in any socialization process for the individual child. The content of such children's literature is also examined for purposes of shedding light on social roles and interactional patterns that are distinctly unique to American culture. A largely thematic method of analysis is employed: thirty-five stories were selected from major children's periodicals dating from the period 1880-1950. Only stories containing the playing of baseball in some form are included and these stories are described through plot explication and identification of primary themes. Five major themes arise here: 1) interpersonal support, 2) individual responsibility, 3) sacrifice in the face of defeat, 4) human modesty, and 5) the value of fair play. Such recurring popular baseball themes are related to structural aspects of the act of baseball playing *viz.,* pacing of the game, configuration in the system of play, and mentorship relationships on the field of play. While no salient trends in the thematic analysis were uncovered, it is demonstrated that the nature of the baseball stories examined was clearly didactic in intent, aimed at transmitting idealized American values through the medium of apparently light and entertaining childhood reading materials.

Golubcow, Saul. Baseball as Metaphor in American Fiction. *Ph.D. Dissertation. The State University of New York at Stony Brook, 1975 (234pp). DAI 36, No. 06, 3712-A (Order no. DDJ75-26148).*

A critical and historical overview of ways in which baseball has been utilized as appropriate metaphor in American fiction, from late 19th-century novels (e.g., Noah Brooks' *The Fairport Nine*) down to the present (especially *The Great American Novel* and *The Natural.*) The earliest metaphorical use of baseball emerged in the visionist period of 1880 to 1919, employing the game not only to relate an exciting sports story but also to honor American values and an American way of life as well. Widespread public disillusionment with the sport in wake of the Black Sox scandal led inevitably to "a more complex and adult revisionist fiction in which not only what occurs on the field is important, but also what transpires off the diamond." Writers such as Ring Lardner and Heywood Broun begin utilizing the national pastime to "accuse, indict, and castigate America for a host of moral failures." Evolution of an emerging notion of the game of baseball as meaningless experience and its players as clowns and morons leads next to non-serious baseball narrative (Thurber and Roth) in which the game "is not so much metaphor as it is gag or slapstick routine." A conclusion of this thesis is that *The Natural* ultimately provides "the total baseball metaphor," a work in which "the romance of the early period, the scorn of the revisionists, and the prankish humor of the non-serious writers all come together" as Malamud utilizes baseball to portray a relationship between a native American hero and a wasteland American society within which he must reside. Golubcow also demonstrates precisely why "with the game as instant metaphor for all of America, a baseball writer is almost destined to fail in covering everything that might be contained in the national experience." He thus maintains that baseball fiction by its very nature is doomed to fall short of its total goal.

Harrison, Walter Lee. Out of Play: Baseball Fiction from Pulp to Art. Ph.D. Dissertation. *University of California, Davis, 1980 (172pp).* DAI 41, No. 09, 4033-A (Order no. DDJ81-05383).

A definition of baseball games as ritualized combat and highly structured and ritualized significant mock actions is provided within the framework of Johann Huizinga's conception of "play elements" in American culture. Each player of the contest maintains a uniquely defined role in which his actions are permanently integrated with those of his teammates; the game provides a perfect balance between the concept of single combat (pitcher versus batter) and a cooperative team competition through which victory can only jointly be obtained. An exceedingly small but articulate body of popular late 19th and early 20th century fiction provides the most appropriate literary expression of baseball's highly formulaic pattern as sport and as artistic subject: "the perilous quest of a family of brothers" to win a pennant in a season-long combat through symbolic warfare, while isolated from the debilitating forces of the everyday world. While Noah Brook's *Our Baseball Club* (the earliest baseball novel) focuses on the unity of team as single-entity, Zane Grey's *The Young Pitcher* introduces the concept of the single baseball hero, whose ultimate test is "to avoid insidious corruption from the world outside the baseball diamond." Popular fictional baseball stars become literary models reflecting sacred American values, yet temptations of American culture increasingly act to corrupt the sterile and idealized baseball world. While Ring Lardner's heroes (especially Jack Keefe in *You Know Me Al*) fail to understand the significance of their actions as baseball heroes, Mark Harris extends Lardner's realistic tradition by providing a hero-narrator (Henry Wiggen) who can realize both potentials and limitations in the baseball star as human hero. Harrison concludes that *The Natural* provides "the most direct expression of the ritualistic importance of baseball" in which "the perilous quest of the baseball season parallels the medieval quest for the Holy Grail." Extending this pattern of baseball as perilous symbolic quest, such other recent important baseball novels as *Universal Baseball Association*, *The Great American Novel*, Philip O'Connor's *Stealing Home*, together extend the exploration of the role of baseball as significant element within American culture.

Knisley, Patrick Allen. The Interior Diamond: Baseball in Twentieth Century American Poetry and Fiction. *Ph.D. Dissertation. University of Colorado at Boulder, 1978 (275pp). DAI 39, No. 05, 2939-A (Order no. DDJ78-20530).*

Aims to merge the historical and aesthetic realities of baseball with the literary, mythological and cultural importance of the fiction and poetry inspired by the game itself. In some of this literature, baseball symbolizes an ordered pastoral realm, outside of time, where motion emerges as ritual; other baseball literature portrays a corrupt world which, as a reflection of American culture itself, has fallen from idyllic promise to moral inferiority and tainted materialism. Baseball has also been utilized as a fictional metaphor for the art and craft of a literary creation itself. Together these thematic and metaphorical uses of the national game constitute a significant tradition within serious American literature of the twentieth century. This study devotes separate chapters to the baseball poetry, the fiction of Ring Lardner, the Henry Wiggen novels of Mark Harris, *The Natural*, *Universal Baseball Association*, *The Great American Novel*, and Herrin's *Rio Loja Ringmaster*. Knisley demonstrates that each of the novelists examined sees baseball as a rich symbolic construct, an entirely unique sport providing its own sense of history, ritual, legend, and native American myth. With a season stretching from early spring to early fall, baseball invites explicit comparison with the seasons of life and growth; its patterns of structured form superimposed upon an artificial landscape furthermore suggest "both the *hortus conclusus* of the pastoral genre and the creation of a work of art."

Kudler, Harvey. Bernard Malamud's "The Natural" and Other Oedipal Analogs in Baseball Fiction. *Ph.D. Dissertation. St. Johns University, 1976 (305pp). DAI 37, No. 09, 5829-A (Order no. DDJ77-01581).*

Aims to explain the surrealistic plot and apparently symbolic characters of Bernard Malamud's *The Natural* in a manner that would properly place this novel within the canon of Malamud's own later fiction, as well as within a tradition of baseball novels developed over the two decades following the appearance of Roy Hobbs. Kudler argues that Malamud built his novel as a symbolic analogue to Sophocles' *Oedipus Rex*, in the same fashion that James Joyce retold the Ulysses legend in the guise of the modern adventures of Leopold Bloom. He contends as well that Malamud constructed a metaphorical baseball novel, utilizing both mythic and Freudian sexual analogs, and in doing so "he created the archetype for the serious baseball novel, describing the game of baseball as primarily an Oedipal duel, with murderous intent on both sides, between a father figure -- the pitcher -- and his young son, the batter at 'home' plate." To support this presumed mythic underpinning of the novel, one chapter fully explicates "ironic metaphors" in *The Natural*, thus deciphering apparent extensive Joycean plot conventions. To demonstrate the presence of a theme of Freudian psycho-sexual guilt as well as a theme of Sophoclean mythic guilt, a second chapter focuses on heavy use of such phallic symbols as Hobbs' bat Wonderboy. Promoted as well is the weighty claim that overall structures and patterns in the game of baseball are inherently Oedipal, and that Malamud was only the first of several baseball novelists "to intuit this phenomenon and interpret it artistically." Other symbolically Oedipal baseball novels are taken to be *Universal Baseball Association*, *Bang the Drum Slowly*, and *The Great American Novel*.

Lass, Terry Russell. Discoveries of Mark Harris and Henry Wiggen. *Ph.D. Dissertation. University of Missouri, 1986 (210pp). DAI 47, No. 10, 3757-A (Order no. DA8701387).*

Argues that Mark Harris' tetralogy of Henry Wiggen baseball novels is a "significant but overlooked achievement in contemporary American fiction." *The Southpaw* (1953) is seen as the best of the Harris novels, one in which Henry Wiggen "serves his apprenticeship as an amateur athlete, enters the world of professional baseball, undergoes a series of physical and moral trials, and emerges with a story to tell and a style to tell it."

OUR WELCOME GUESTS: AMERICA'S CHAMPION BASEBALL PLAYERS.

Henry Wiggen's personal journey of self-exploration and self-discovery is examined in detail throughout three chapters which review the middle novels of the sequence, *Bang the Drum Slowly* (1956) and *A Ticket for A Seamstitch* (1957.) A separate chapter traces Henry's widening social consciousness, his acceptance of the possibilities of social community, and his emergence as an important fictional hero of the '50s. A final chapter is devoted to the more recent revival of the Henry Wiggen figure in the 1979 novel *It Looked Like Forever*, as well as drawing critical evaluations of Harris' baseball tetralogy from a number of unusual and diverse contemporary sources.

Merrell, David Boles. "Take Me Out to the Ballgame": Baseball as Determinant in Selected American Fiction. *Ph.D. Dissertation. Texas A&M University, 1979 (196pp). DAI 40, No. 12, 6281-A (Order no. DDJ80-11975).*

While novels representing serious baseball fiction have provided several distinctive types of narrative perspective, in all such novels "baseball serves as a determinant of microcosm, character, structure, action, and ethics." Merrell illustrates this thesis with the following exemplary novels and competing narrative modes: Lardner's *You Know Me Al* (a first-person epistolary novel); Harris' trilogy of Henry Wiggen's stories (first-person peripheral viewpoint); *The Natural* (third-person omniscient narrative); and *Universal Baseball Assocation* (metafictional novel utilizing a central reflector and eventual unmediated reflection of the fictional world). The ordered social world of baseball provides a perfect analogue and microcosm for larger American society; baseball novelists like Lardner, Harris, and Malamud place fictional players and teams within actual major league settings, while Roth and Coover create fictional leagues parallel to the features of real professional baseball. Characters populating these novels are drawn from stereotypes of the baseball hero, in the model of Babe Ruth, Joe Jackson, or other representative heroic or tragic (or even comic) real-life baseball figures. The seasonal cycle of baseball also provides a determinant for the time frame of narrative action: "the feeling of baseball time as determined by the individual game suggests the timeless past and the timeless future." Narrative action and a moral-ethical framework for such fictive action are also strictly determined by parameters of the actual game of baseball. If action in the baseball novel falls within the bounds of plausible or recorded baseball history (is in line with past statistics and baseball legends), then realism is achieved within the novel; if action and event are improbable, then the novel evolves into fantasy. Baseball's narrowly and precisely defined ethics (e.g., codes exist for players' actions, and certain actions such as stealing the catcher's signs are condoned) provide the means for judging character and action within the baseball story. The novels of Lardner, Harris, Malamud and Roth demonstrate the degree to which the microcosmic world of baseball efficiently functions as a determining vehicle in the structuring of American fiction.

Reynolds, Charles Dewey Hilles. Baseball as the Material of Fiction. *Ph.D. Dissertation. University of Nebraska, 1974 (272pp). DAI 35, No. 05, 3005-A (Order no. DDJ74-23931).*

Although rapid growth of baseball popularity in the middle nineteenth century led to a labeling of the sport as the "national pastime" as early as 1850, it was a full century later before serious baseball fiction caught the nation's attention. Reynolds explains that adult baseball fiction appeared precisely at a time when the game was being systematically divorced from its adoring public through extensive commercialism (through "big-business baseball" with its TV coverage, elaborate farm systems, and crass commercialism.) By 1950 adults had taken over the child's game and television had transformed "the country game" into a big-city business which resulted in "a distant activity viewed in a small box." Reynolds focuses on three aspects of the literary handling of baseball within serious adult treatments after 1950. The *sociological aspect* reflects idealism concerning the national pastime as melting-pot: city-country distinctions are paramount in baseball fiction because "a country player's triumphs assert the American Dream," while socio-economic barriers such as race are rarely mentioned in baseball fiction (the issue not even being considered until Eliot Asinof's *Man on Spikes*.) The *imaginative aspect* focuses on potential fictional means of overcoming limits of probability in treating a sport based so heavily on the mathematical boundaries of a playing field and on the game's relevant statistics. *The Natural* is taken to illustrate how the serious baseball novelist has utilized baseball's own inherent mythology, rather than trying to create an original mythology for baseball fiction. The *moral aspect* explores the problem of "ideal versus real," with *The Southpaw* taken as the first novel "to show baseball's moral dichotomy seriously as an issue for the player," and Malamud's story extending the conflict to the issue of "the fixed game" and the nature of heroism. Writers of baseball fiction before 1950 had focused largely upon play on the field. But television has unraveled baseball from the fabric of American life, and "with aesthetic distance and separation of the game in literature from the game on the field, baseball has now become a worthy subject for a serious American fiction."

Smith, Leverett T., Jr. The American Dream and the National Game. *Ph.D. Dissertation. University of Minnesota, Minneapolis, 1970 (553pp). DAI 32, No. 03, 1530-A (Order no. 718267).*

Aims to demonstrate similarities between literary culture and American culture at large; this is attempted through analysis of both literary documents (literary masterpieces and materials from the field of professional sports, especially from baseball) and historical documents from the realm of popular culture, in the effort to see if both hold political and social values in common. Smith's thesis is summarized as follows: "that the concept of play, which led a perilous existence in the literature of the 19th century and early 20th century because of the predominance of the work ethic, has, since the end of World War I, begun to gain the kind of status the work ethic once had, and that this ethic is now equally visible in literary works and in the world of professional sports as an ethic-alternative to the supposed ethics of the commercial democratic society as a whole." Baseball-related sections include a chapter on the writings of Ring Lardner, a chapter on the evolution of professional baseball between 1919 and 1922 and the impact of the Black Sox on baseball's relationship to a commercial society, and a section studying the public images of Ty Cobb and Babe Ruth and their crucial relations to shifting values of a commercialized democracy.

2. Dissertations on Baseball in American Culture and American History

Furst, R. Terry. The Image of Professional Baseball: The Sport Press and the Formation of Ideas About Baseball in Nineteenth Century America. *Ph.D. Dissertation. New School for Social Research, 1986 (363pp). DAI 47, No. 06, 2323-A (Order no. DA8616022).*

Describes and analyzes the process by which the collective image of professional baseball was formed, tracing both negation and affirmation of ideas within the popular sports press which worked to impede or promote the growth of professional baseball from its role as recreational pastime to its emergence as a popular spectator sport in 19th-century America. Furst demonstrates that the public image of baseball fostered through the sporting press was never a stable one: conflict arose from competing images of an older, social-recreational approach to playing the game and a newer and much more competitive professional style of play. Such important early baseball events as the Cincinnati Red Stockings tour of 1869 are traced through their press accounts, with attention given equally to editorial commentaries, evaluative descriptions by sports reporters, and judgmental reader-letters to the editors of major dailies. It is clear that "the image of professional baseball grew, not as a unitary concept, but rather as a composite of attributes stemming from an interactive complex . . . including both reportage and reading of baseball matters in the sport press, discussion of baseball within social and occupational networks, game attendance and changing values (sic) toward work and play."

Goldstein, Warren Jay. Playing for Keeps: A History of American Baseball, 1857-1876. Ph.D. Dissertation. Yale University, 1983 (304pp). DAI 44, No. 09, 2808-A (Order no. DEQ83-29232).

Demonstrates through baseball -- the principal if not the only major spectator sport of the late 19th century -- the changing and emerging relationships between the experiences of work and play. What results by the turn of the century is the unique notion that these were in fact distinct spheres of human activity. Because the organized game of baseball first emerged from and flourished in a culture and community of skilled urban craftsmen, the language of the game rapidly became barely distinguishable from the language of productive labor; the result was also that players as well as commentators on the game "stressed the skillful play which produced ballfield victories." A central focus of this dissertation is the profound transformation of baseball (from club-based fraternal game featuring skilled craftsmen to entertainment business supported by gate receipts) which transpired during the two decades between 1857 and 1876. Club management and sport commentators of this period first introduced the language and practices of "management" and an inevitable result was that relationships between team management and players evolved to parallel that between employers and their workers in all other phases of the American business community. Founding of the National League in 1876 was the first formal association of clubs rather than players, and this action formalized the existing trend toward institutionalizing the new commercial structure of American baseball. But as baseball emerged as an institution of commercialized leisure activity it also maintained an ideology of "pure recreation" (the myth of the "democratic pastime" now far removed from the anxieties of the daily workplace); this dichotomy in baseball's public image grew out of an internal development of the game from pure club sport of amateur flavor into profitable business, replete with its own highly specialized professional workplace (the ballpark).

Haven, Jeffrey Lawrence. Baseball: The Origins and Development of the Game to 1903. Ed.D. Dissertation. Brigham Young University, 1979 (232pp). DAI 40, No. 02, 1027-A (Order no. DDJ79-18437).

Focusing on the development of the institution of baseball within 19th-century American society, this work narrates the historical evolution of the sport from its American origins through the mergers of the National and American Leagues in 1903. Haven emphasizes both a narrative account, which will interest sports enthusiasts, as well as more analytical assessment, which provides significant discussion for scholars of American

LARGEST WEEKLY CIRCULATION IN AMERICA

TIP TOP WEEKLY

AN IDEAL PUBLICATION
FOR THE AMERICAN YOUTH

By subscription $2.50 per year. Entered as Second-class Matter at the N. Y. Post Office, by STREET & SMITH, 79-89 Seventh Ave., N. Y.

No. 541   NEW YORK, AUGSUT 25, 1906.   Price, Five Cents

DICK MERRIWELL'S HEART

or BREAKING THE HARD LUCK STREAK

By BURT L. STANDISH

"Only a hundred dollars, Mr. Silkshaw?" cried Dick, laughing derisively and flinging the crumpled bill into the man's face. "When you want to buy me bring me a bale of these!"

social history. Historically accurate accounts are provided for the birth of the game in its American version, expansion and development of baseball from the first amateur clubs to touring professional teams, the growth in professionalism under the auspices of the National Baseball League, commercialization within the business of professional baseball, and dominant players and teams of the game's first half-century.

Hull, Adrian Louis. The Linguistic Accommodation of a Cultural Innovation as Illustrated by the Game of Baseball in the Spanish Language of Puerto Rico. *Ph.D. Dissertation. Columbia University, 1963 (399pp). DAI 25, No. 12, 7256 (Order no. 64-09884).*

Since no Spanish-speaking countries have an indigenous counterpart to the North American game of baseball, adoption of this game by the native culture of Puerto Rico caused linguistic difficulties of considerable impact, especially in terms of the words and expressions necessary to describe adequately the objects, actions, practices, and events of the game. Methods are explored by which a native Puerto Rican population resolved this problem both through utilization of native Spanish-language resources as well as borrowings from American English speech. Hull identifies and also defines linguistic interference emerging from language-contact situations involving the importation of American baseball to the Puerto Rican island nation; the study is largely synchronic in its focus on Puerto Rican baseball language over the four previous years, including the lexical, phonological, morphological, syntactic, and orthographic levels of usage. A principal source for oral language was the recording of radio broadcasts of baseball games; written materials were gathered from local newspaper accounts of game results and game action. No effort was made, however, to distinguish between social, regional, colloquial, or literary levels of language usage, it being assumed here that baseball attracts an audience from all walks of life and that those following the game utilize common expressions and a highly specialized vocabulary also common to the sport. Four central observations summarize the observed language-change phenomena which has accompanied the cultural innovation of baseball in Puerto Rico: 1) evidence exists for an accelerated language change in the Puerto Rican Spanish used in connection with the game of baseball; 2) evidence exists for deviations from the norm on all linguistic levels (phonological, syntactic, etc.) in Spanish employed to discuss baseball; 3) American English baseball language exerts a strong influence on Puerto Rican Spanish baseball language; and 4) evidence suggests that some deviations in Spanish baseball language are not at all due to any linguistic influence of American baseball language, but rather to natural evolution within the Spanish language forms.

Kammer, David John. Take Me Out to the Ballgame: American Cultural Values as Reflected in the Architectural Evolution and Criticism of the Modern Baseball Stadium. *Ph.D. Dissertation. The University of New Mexico, Albuquerque, 1982 (407pp). DAI 43, No. 10, 3356-A (Order no. DEP83-04350).*

Elaborates the unique thesis that "using traditional modes of architectural criticism and then expanding them to encompass popular cultural tastes, one can trace the changes in the ballpark as reflecting changes in American society at large, particularly in the areas of urban demography, transportation, and mass entertainment." Kammer suggests that while the urban baseball stadium has long been an American fixture, no one has previously examined any serious social implications of changes in architectural style, construction technology, or urban location. Construction of three representative ball parks (Yankee Stadium, Dodger Stadium, and the Houston Astrodome) is explored as a significant reflection of important advances in building technology evolving through three distinct generations of such concrete and steel stadia. A surprising thesis results: with emphasis on middle-class access to the stadium, more luxurious spectator facilities, and increasing standardization in playing-field appearance and dimensions, the more modern baseball stadium can be taken to reflect "a more homogenized, mobile and spectacle-oriented society" than that which preceded World War I.

Voigt, David Quentin. Cash and Glory: The Commercialization of Major League Baseball as a Sports Spectacular. *D.S.S. Dissertation. Syracuse University, 1962 (505pp). DAI 24, No. 01, 425-A (Order no. 63-3637).*

Traces the history of baseball as a by-product of large-scale industrialization and of a related and historically unique problem of increased leisure time available to working-class masses. Voigt portrays baseball from its earliest appearance as an amateur sport for gentlemanly participants, through its transformation by the final decade of the nineteenth century into a highly commercialized sporting spectacle providing significant new leisure outlets for the masses of middle-class urbanites. Some primary sources of data for this study are personal correspondences, books, and other records authored by such participants in 19th-century baseball as managers, players, club administrators, and professional sports journalists. Several important observations and descriptions are also drawn from sporting journals and magazines, baseball guides and manuals of the period, and reporting in hometown newspapers on each pennant-winning team of the era. Baseball is treated from a largely sociological frame of reference; the unique American national pastime is here described as a newly emerging type of socially significant leisure-time outlet, as "a sports spectacular catering to the psychological needs of increasingly urbanized Americans."

NOTE: In addition to the seventeen dissertations discussed in this report, two additional early projects also exist which pre-date all published *DAI* catalog abstracts. These pioneer non-abstracted dissertations are perhaps the most widely cited of those studies treating historical topics; certainly they are the best-known among scholars not yet familiar with the larger inventory of baseball dissertations.

Nichols, Edward J. An Historical Dictionary of Baseball Terminology. *Ph.D. Dissertation. The Pennsylvania State University, 1939 (112pp). DAI 2, 196 (no DAI abstract provided -- Order no. 00-00127).*

Detailed historical accounts are provided for "origins" of most of the terms, labels, and concepts of the national pastime, with significant insight provided into the evolution of our national game against the social backdrop of nineteenth-century industrialization. This work is now mainly significant from a bibliographical or historical perspective, being the first major academic study of baseball carried out in a college English Department.

Seymour, Harold. The Rise of Major League Baseball to 1891. *Ph.D. Dissertation. Cornell University, 1956 (659pp). DAI 16, 2145 (no DAI abstract provided — Order no. 0019159).*

A detailed history of baseball's first half-century, this is the earliest draft of parts of Seymour's pioneer research later published as volume one (*Baseball, The Early Years*, Oxford University Press, 1960) of his landmark two-volume social history of the national pastime. Little is found here that is not later available, in more polished form, in the book version treating the same material. There is still, however, the most painstaking academic history of the game's early decades.